FINDING MY TWENTY-FIVE

FINDING MY TWENTY-FIVE

The Prime of Your Life Is Now

Wayne Beck

NEW DEGREE PRESS

FINDING MY TWENTY-FIVE

The Prime of Your Life Is Now

ISBN

978-1-63676-805-2   *Paperback*

978-1-63730-237-8   *Kindle Ebook*

978-1-63730-248-4   *Digital Ebook*

For Jenny,

Forever together,

Forever yours.

CONTENTS

———

*I look to the future because that's where
I'm going to spend the rest of my life.*

—GEORGE BURNS

INTRODUCTION

———

Tim Ballard was an ambitious twentysomething preparing for a future career in federal law enforcement. He graduated with a 4.0 GPA in political science and Spanish and earned a master's in international politics. He loved his work as a federal agent.[1]

But it was not an easy job.

One challenge with working in law enforcement is learning how to manage your emotions when you see people suffering because of vile acts committed by others. Tim sought to find that balance of separating his own life from the emotional burden and anguish of what he witnessed in the course of his duties. There is no filter, such as there would be watching a video documentary. You try to put things out of your mind. You try to tell yourself repeatedly there's only so much you can do.

One day he chanced on a newsfeed that would change the course of his life. A small child was kidnapped in Haiti.

---

1   Lynn Packer, "Tim Ballard's Mission"," *American Crime Journal,* August 6, 2020.

A devastating earthquake struck Haiti in January 2010. Just a few weeks before the earthquake, on December 6, 2009, Guesno Mardy of Port-au-Prince had just finished conducting church services. Suddenly his three-year-old son Gardy was gone.[2] Witnesses saw a former employee of Guesno take Gardy away on a motorcycle. The kidnapper solicited the assistance of child traffickers to try to arrange for a ransom. The kidnapper was caught, but Gardy was still missing and presumed to have been trafficked.[3]

The news article Tim saw included a picture of Guesno Mardy. The picture shows Guesno cleaning up rubble and helping people injured in the earthquake. Tim kept remembering the picture of Guesno, and the story kept coming to mind, despite his efforts to put it aside. That father's son had been kidnapped. The only search going on was conducted by Guesno as he wandered the streets at night listening for his son's voice.

As the story continued to haunt Tim, a feeling he had to do something was working within his soul. His feelings prompted him to contact the boy's father. He arranged for Guesno to come and meet him. He didn't know beforehand what he would say or do.

In their meeting Guesno asked, "Can you imagine going to bed at night knowing one of your children's beds is empty? And not knowing where that child is?" Without hesitation, Tim said, "I will never stop 'til we find your son." He had

---

2   Cheryl Karr L., "Searching for the One: Gardy Mardy," *O.U.R. Stories,* July 17, 2014.

3   Operation Underground Railroad, "Gardy's Story (Part 4 of 8)," *O.U.R. Stories,* June 19, 2020.

been impressed to make a promise he was not in position to fulfill because his employer couldn't send him to work a case in Haiti.[4]

After consulting his wife, she was acting on faith when she told him the answer was simple: "You quit your job and you raise money. You go find that little boy because you made a promise."[5]

Tim Ballard turned in his badge. There was no turning back.

It was time for action. He had to get support, raise funds, and put together a team to go to work finding this young boy.

The challenge was overwhelming. He was following Abraham Lincoln's admonition given to Congress in 1862, "The occasion is piled high with difficulty and we must rise with the occasion."[6] Confident in his inspiration that pathways would open up, donors stepped up to fund a rescue operation. Others came to form a rescue team. He founded and is now the CEO of Operation Underground Railroad (O.U.R.).[7]

His efforts and diligence in his twenties prepared him for a change of course that continues to free people from the shackles of slavery. Tim's story reminded me of other stories

4   Timothy Ballard, *Slave Stealers: True Accounts of Slave Rescues Then and Now.* (Salt Lake City, Rockwell Group Inc., 2018), 32-33.

5   Tony Robbins' Facebook Page, "Tony Robbins Interviews Tim Ballard, Whose Mission Is To End...," Video, 36:25.

6   Abraham Lincoln, "Abraham Lincoln Quotes," *Goodreads,* accessed January 23, 2021.

7   Operation Underground Railroad, "The Team," accessed March 28, 2021.

of inspiring people who broke away from the norm to find or create a new or expanded purpose, far beyond any previous expectations.

Tim's story is one example of how people open new paths in life by inspiration, necessity, or both. In this book you will see twentysomethings who bust through stereotypes that might otherwise hold them back, and how people of all generations can fully optimize attributes and opportunities at any age.

As a police officer at Brigham Young University (BYU), I hired and supervised several dozen student security officers (twentysomethings) over the course of my career. I found them to be highly productive, enthused, and competent. They have gone on to many successful careers. I frequently received phone calls from graduate school professors and corporate leaders thanking me for whatever part I had in preparing my employees for the real world. The fact is they came to me well-prepared. I only provided them the opportunity to continue building experience along their paths. I was amazed with their work ethic and integrity. My recruiting and selection process brought in the best prepared employees possible. I expected a lot from them. That was easy for me, because they expected a great deal of themselves.

I tried not to lose sight of the fact that being a twentysomething is not the same for everyone. There were still a lot of twentysomethings without a compass and some without a rudder. The third decade of life can be a challenging time. Looking back on your own twenties, some tough issues may seem trivial now. It's tempting to look at current twentysomethings and wonder what's wrong with them. You may be perplexed when you see your adult children missing what you thought were key markers of adulthood, such as finishing school, getting married, settling on a career path, moving out of their parents' house, or becoming financially self-sufficient.

A *New York Times Magazine* article from a decade ago reports one-third of twentysomethings move to a new residence yearly; 40 percent move back home at least once.[8] Some parents call their kids boomerang children. We don't realize how much external factors influence individual circumstances or decisions. There may be good reasons for their fear and indecisiveness.

There is a tendency to criticize other groups when we haven't taken time to recognize the environment they are living in. We may puff our chest out and criticize adult children living at home, or we can help them create the circumstances to courageously move forward in life. Adult children living at home is not a new phenomenon.

Due to the economy, at the end of the Great Depression 48 percent of young adults ages eighteen to twenty-nine were living in the home of one or both parents. That number dropped to 29 percent by 1960, then continued to trend upward. It reached 47 percent in February 2020 just as the COVID-19 pandemic was about to let loose on the economy. By July of 2020, that number reached 52 percent. For the first time in

---

8   Robin Marantz Henig, "What Is It About 20-Somethings?" *New York Times Magazine*, August 18, 2009.

the United States, over half of eighteen to twenty-nine-year-olds were living with their parents.[9]

The COVID-19 pandemic has been hard on twentysomethings, especially those younger than twenty-five who typically work part-time and lower skill level jobs. For those in college, there was even more uncertainty. "Among all adults who moved due to the pandemic, 23 percent said the most important reason was because their college campus had closed, and 18 percent said it was due to job loss or other financial reasons."[10]

That doesn't mean adult children should just settle in because life was hard on the outside. Whatever path you choose, the real choice is the choice to get moving, to create momentum, and to drive you through changing circumstances.

Clinical psychologist Dr. Meg Jay declares "claiming your twenties is one of the simple yet most transformative things you can do for your work, your happiness, even for the world."[11] After years of counseling twentysomethings, she recognizes the importance of the advantages available in your twenties. She has seen what she considers to be too many people come into her practice feeling regret for slacking their way through and missing tremendous opportunities. She indicates during this decade your brain rewires itself and caps off its second and last growth spurt.

---

9   Richard Fry, Jeffrey S. Passel and D'Vera Cohn, "A Majority of Young Adults in the U.S. Live with Their Parents for the First Time since the Great Depression," *Pew Research Center,* September 4, 2020.

10 Ibid.

11 *TED,* "Why 30 Is Not the New 20," May 13, 2013, video, 14:49.

I worry that supposing your brain ceases developing by age thirty may lead you to believe you are on a decline, that you've completely missed the boat. I wonder if some clients come away feeling too much regret for "slacking" through their twenties and feel hopeless. They look around at others who, at least on the surface, appear to have it all together. I have heard many twentysomethings express these very concerns.

I have spent my life listening deeply for understanding. This has been an essential asset for me in unravelling the circumstances around criminal activity or discovering why a sixteen-year-old is addicted to theft. I have also listened to many share their feelings after their coaching, therapy, or counseling sessions. Listening is the greatest teacher. It is also a great tool for healing.

I don't have a degree in psychology, but I know how to listen. My MA in Spanish linguistics has refined my listening skills. Language is the gift that separates us from all other species. I specialize in the study of seventeenth century legal depositions and court testimonies from Spain, Cuba, and the coast of Ecuador. Most of the testimonies I study are of common workers, most of them illiterate. They give their statement orally while a scribe records their words. As I read, centuries later, it is as though I personally hear the witnesses speak. In 1689, a teenage sailor spoke of his tremendous fear when he went out to sea for the first time. I felt his fear; I still feel it, and I'm still listening.

I am inspired by the people whose voices made this book possible. I invite you to listen to them and learn from their stories.

Often as twentysomethings you are under outside pressure to make choices and "good" decisions. You may become deflated when things don't work out according to somebody's "norm." Listening to others can be good therapy as you sort out your own life.

The potential is very real for working your way to a career and finding it's not satisfying, or for finding the economy has shifted and you're not needed there. When my friend Sean heard I was writing a book about twentysomethings, he sent me a message asking me to remember those who are in their fourth decade with little hope of advancement. I know Sean and am confident he will build on his experiences and continue to move forward. The fact he recognizes feeling stuck is a motivation to find a path to break free. In this book, you will meet people who have gone out and established their own unique paths. Sometimes they're motivated by prompting, often by circumstance.

According to a 2016 survey by the Society for Human Resource Management, 38 percent of employees in the US are very satisfied with their jobs. Fifty-one percent are satisfied to a lesser degree (but perhaps not feeling fulfilled in their work). With 89 percent satisfied or somewhat satisfied, one out of ten are dissatisfied.[12] I'm concerned for that "one."

External or unpredictable factors can throw off the best plans. What if the economy tanks right when you graduate? As we see with the effects of the COVID-19 pandemic, things can

---

12   Christina Lee, "2017 Employee Job Satisfaction and Engagement: The Doors of Opportunity Are Open," *Society for Human Resource Management,* April 24, 2017.

change unexpectedly and sometimes very suddenly. However, you never lose the freedom to make choices and to change directions. Along with the world around us, we are always evolving.

For years I've mingled with twentysomethings from many backgrounds and with a variety of aspirations. There are many paths to success, and numerous perceptions of what success is. In this book you will see the value of creating and following your own path in your own time. This book taps into the experiences and attributes of people in their twenties. As important as your twenties are, you are not locked in.

My grandma was a dedicated mother of six during her twenties but had additional ambitions and goals. Grandma Aline wrote and published romance stories for magazines while she was working at the Brown Derby Restaurant and raising a family. She also wanted to serve as a nurse. After her bus rides home from work and after putting her family to bed, she would sit down at her typewriter. Then, at age fifty-one, she fulfilled her dream of being a nurse. After a short career caring for others, she put her skills into practice to care for my grandfather during his decline while suffering from Alzheimer's. She took on that new challenge as a caregiver. Though his memory failed, she continued to learn, thrive, and prosper in her advanced years.

Dr. Meg Jay notes the last growth spurt of the brain occurs during your twenties. However, the brain does not fully stop developing and adapting to new needs and stimuli. In looking at the topic, Ferris Jabr of *Scientific American* discovered research showing that, though at a slower pace, neuroplasticity continues well beyond your twenties. He concludes, "The human brain is not a soufflé that gradually expands over time and finally finishes 'baking' at age thirty. Yes, we can identify and label periods of dramatic development—or windows of heightened plasticity—but that should not eclipse the fact that the brain changes throughout life."[13]

To qualify as a taxi driver in London, you are required to learn every nook and cranny of the city. According to the Public Carriage Office, 98 percent of London taxi drivers are over age thirty. To certify, the drivers are put through a rigorous study and training program to gain a thorough knowledge of the layout of the city. These drivers study, practice, and are regularly tested for three to four years before they qualify for certification.

Katherine Woollett and Eleanor Maguire of the Institute of Neurology of University College, London, measured significant brain development in taxi drivers completing the certification. Average-IQ adults trained for four years to learn the complex layout of London's streets. "In those who qualified, acquisition of an internal spatial representation of London was associated with a selective increase in gray matter (GM) volume in their posterior hippocampi and concomitant changes to their memory profile. No structural brain changes were observed in trainees who failed to qualify or in control participants."[14]

---

13   Ferris Jabr, "The Neuroscience of 20-Somethings," *Scientific American*, August 29, 2012.

14   Katherine Woollett and Eleanor Maguire, "Acquiring 'the Knowledge' of London's Layout Drives Structural Brain Changes," *Current Biology* 21, no. 24 (2011): 2109–2114.

If you are intentional in your goals and what you want to be, you are not doomed, no matter how old you are. Your challenges may be different at different ages, but there are always challenges in life, at any age. You can always direct your trajectory and, as couched in the title of one of Wayne Dyer's books, *Manifest Your Destiny*.[15]

I wrote this book based on my vast and deep experience with twentysomethings. During my career as a police officer at Brigham Young University, I never missed a home football game. I never watched a game either; I was working. I worked one hundred fifty consecutive home games as a police officer. I still remember the feeling of the power of fifty thousand fans energizing the stadium at my first game. A vast array of staff and volunteers worked to support the teams and harness that energy into a meaningful and positive experience for everyone.

The realization I had been in the university environment for a long time came one day when it occurred to me I had been working those games since before any of the current players were even born. It was a similar experience working basketball games. Not too long ago, a father and son approached the basketball arena. In the same instant each of them yelled out to me, "Hey, Officer Wayne!" Then they each asked, "He's your friend, too?"

Among the skills needed to develop effective police work are listening and observing while assessing the totality of circumstances. I've missed the mark a few times when I missed

15 Wayne Dyer, *Manifest Your Destiny: The Nine Spiritual Principles for Getting Everything You Want* (New York, Harper Collins, 1997), title page.

something or got too caught up in the processes to recognize what was happening on an individual basis or a deeper level. We're all learning together. If it wasn't for these experiences, I wouldn't be where I am today. I wrote this book to continue to learn from and serve teenagers reaching for their twenties, and twentysomethings building themselves into the future for a bountiful and productive path through the decades.

My first training for police work and learning from twentysomethings started very early on at Disneyland. In the 1960s, admission was $6.95, the same cost as a pair of new shrink-to-fit Levi's jeans. I was born the same year Disneyland opened and made my first visit by age two. As a family, we went often, especially on rainy days when the lines for the rides were shorter.

What did I learn at Disneyland? Quite a lot, it turns out. My mom was a great mentor for teaching me the observation skills ideal for a future police officer.

At Disneyland, we would all meet up at a specific location on Main Street at designated times to regroup and keep track of each other. While waiting with Mom on the bench, she would often comment on what people might be thinking as they walked by. She taught me how to guess what their conversations might be by how they walked, their clothes, or the souvenirs they were carrying. It was really a lot of fun. I had no idea I was building policing skills that would later help me sense danger, anticipate people's intentions and perceive their efforts to deceive.

Years later in, 1981, I graduated from Utah State University. I was trained and ready to work in the horticulture industry.

I had my degree in hand. The economic timing wasn't to my advantage. I had heard in 1979, two years before my graduation, the job placement for my major was over 80 percent. By the time I graduated it was around 3 percent. The average starting pay was less than half of what it had been.

I worked a lot of hours, sometimes up to eighty hours, for very little pay. Then, out of the blue, I was offered a job as a commercial air conditioning mechanic. The pay and benefits put me on track. I enjoyed the work, and the crew I worked with was amazing. I changed my path and began searching for my future path beyond air conditioning.

My friend Ron was a police officer and took me out on patrol a few times. I saw it as a potential to impact lives in a positive way and to change the world, at least for some people. With a sluggish economy and people looking for work, getting the job was competitive. On July 24, 1984, I raised my arm and swore to uphold the Constitution of the United States of America and the Constitution of the State of California.

Some of my friends challenged my decision to become a police officer by saying things like, "You're just one person, you can't change the world." Others warned witnessing so much sadness and tragedy in people's lives would make me calloused and cold. I promised myself and prayed every day I would have a lasting positive effect on someone's life. I put the hiring board on notice that if I became too calloused or found the job separated me from who I wanted to be or from my family, I would leave the career. My prayers were and continue to be answered as it relates to having the ability to impact someone's life every day.

Nearing my thirty-year mark in the profession, I was leading the design and management of the security systems at Brigham Young University. With no warning, I was transferred away from the assignment I had poured so much into. It was a sign to me, an opportunity to build a new path.

I was working out in the gym when suddenly I felt something, though I couldn't identify what. I told my partner David Griffin to wait a minute. I told him I needed to do something. He asked me what I needed to do, but I didn't know. It was a feeling. Out of nowhere, a man who introduced himself as Ben Hardy appeared. He had seen me at another gym, though I didn't remember him. When he saw me on this day, he received a strong impression to talk to me.

After a few moments of conversation, he offered his services as a life coach for a few weeks before he was to leave town to work on a PhD program in psychology. At half my age, a twentysomething, he sensed where I was in life. One of the first things he asked me was if I was ready to break those golden handcuffs that held me bound. I knew if I accepted him into my life, the life I was accustomed to would change forever. Welcome to twenty-five.

Ever since that moment, I realized I had surrounded myself with twentysomethings most of my life. I had been watching and learning all those years how successful twentysomethings operate. It was my turn to apply those observations in my own life during my fifties. I feel compelled to encourage others to apply the same principles that can free anyone to be what they want to be and accomplish what they know in their heart is right.

Changing direction and building a new future are common for twentysomethings, but it is certainly not reserved for them alone.

Now in my sixties, I continue to experience and create change. You will see more examples of how unplanned circumstances may, at first glance, appear to take away your freedom, but in reality set the table for new opportunities. I felt a surge of freedom when I left my police career. I planned to teach college Spanish classes and do consulting for security systems. However, fate pushed those things aside.

As soon as I left the police department, my mother-in-law's condition as an Alzheimer's patient rapidly deteriorated. I have since been very confined to my home to assist in her care.

We've seen how Tim Ballard followed his promptings and changed course and how my grandmother began fulfilling a dream in her fifties. Even though they are well beyond their twenties, London taxi drivers show us the brain can continue to adapt and grow if diligently challenged. Your ability to make positive changes does not stop at any specific age.

This book is for twentysomethings who are ready to maximize all the advantages available during what should be an exciting time in life.

This book is also for anyone beyond their twenties who feels it's time to re-invent their present and future. No matter how insurmountable the barriers seem to be, your life is still malleable. You can still make and execute decisions.

Teens will find strength and confidence in this book. Sometimes teens are ignored or pushed aside because they are typically in such an active discovery mode. There is no better time to build on your successes and learn from your setbacks than now.

There are two powerful forces at work as you forge your path. On the one hand, opportunities and benefits provide you with an unlimited supply of tools and resources to create and accomplish your goals. On the other hand, obstacles and traps seem to block the way. Those obstacles can defeat you for a time. The experience of breaking free and overcoming qualify you for even greater opportunities and progression.

By the time you've reached your twenties, you've experienced triumphs and failures. You've overcome obstacles and are likely dealing with significant challenges as you enter that important decade. You are gaining better judgment, more wisdom, and greater understanding. Finding your twenty-five is a matter of perspective.

We've seen how the father of a kidnapped child inspired a government agent to change his path to save countless others. Adapting to her circumstances, my grandmother reached her goals and became a nurse. The taxi drivers of London have shown we can continue to learn and grow our brains well into adulthood.

The advantages of living in your twenties are available to you no matter how old you are or what condition you're in. If you are like most people, you'll find you have more flexibility and freedom than you realized. Here, you'll hear stories of people who have and continue to overcome real obstacles. You can share these stories to lift and teach anyone who may benefit from recognizing there is hope and there are solutions. You will see how people work with others and tap into unlimited resources. There are different ways to react to challenges, adversity, and trauma, as well as to new and unexpected opportunities. The concept is to create the success you desire.

Finding My Twenty-Five is an exercise of discovery to prepare you to find the tools you will need to be who you choose to be.

I do not promise you a red sports car surrounded by a lush landscape with two palm trees. If that is your goal, you can find the path to get you there. You are free to choose your path and adapt it to changes in circumstances or changing goals as you feel prompted.

The purpose of this book is not to define your success or to give you a road map to a prescribed destination I choose for you. My goal is to share stories and insights to inspire you to direct your path to who you want to be and who you want to become.

PART 1

TIME TO THRIVE

CHAPTER 1

TWENTYSOMETHINGS

"You are the new greatest generation."

—GENERAL DAVID PETRAEUS

When I became a cop, I learned the adage, "You don't know what you've got until you've got it." The wisdom in the saying was to be prepared for anything, not to be overanxious of what you thought was something big, or caught off guard if it turned out to be much more. The person who calls the police may not have all the facts. In some cases, the caller doesn't know if a man who collapsed on the street was assaulted. In others, the caller will embellish a story and say the suspect has a gun just to get a quicker response. Someone may flag you down. Initially, you don't know what it's about. You look and listen and make observations as you go.

The same principle can apply to psychotherapists. You don't know what you've got until you've got it. While in her twenties, Meg Jay was in a PhD program studying clinical psychology at the University of California Berkeley. She was about to see her first client, a twentysomething like herself. She didn't know why her first client had made an appointment. She didn't know what she had. A twenty-six-year-old female client named Alex came in, plopped on the couch, and kicked off her flats. I'm guessing she felt quite comfortable, like this was a routine visit for her. Meg listened as Alex said she wanted to talk about guy problems. Meg was relieved to hear that; a fellow classmate's first client was an arsonist.[16]

Dr. Jay would listen as Alex came into each session with new, sometimes amusing stories. But nothing was changing. Her client was convinced society had changed, that thirty was the new twenty, that there was no rush about anything. Meg met with her supervisor, who encouraged her to push Alex beyond her comfort zone. What initially appeared easy compared to dealing with an arsonist became the opposite. Meg said she had a lightbulb moment at one point. She realized your twenties constitute the sweet spot in life, when you can and should build your life.[17]

Dr. Jay describes the third decade as a critical time in life, "a time when the things we do—and the things we don't do—will have an enormous impact across years and even generations to come."[18] According to the *Merriam-Webster Dictionary*, the term "twentysomething" began to appear in 1990, defined as someone having an age of generally twenty to twenty-nine.[19] It was popularized in the same year on the cover of *Time Magazine*.[20]

---

16   *TED,* "Meg Jay: Why 30 Is Not the New 20," May 13, 2013, video, 14:49.

17   Ibid.

18   "Meg Jay, About Page," Meg Jay, accessed September 2, 2020.

19   *Merriam-Webster,* s.v. "twentysomething," accessed January 11, 2021.

20   David Gross and Sophronia Scott, "Proceeding with Caution," *Time* Vol. 136, No. 3 (July 16, 1990): 56-62.

Twentysomethings seem to have a reputation of, or rather are stereotyped by society as, having a myriad of issues that hold them back. Yet so many of them break through and seem to soar.

Twentysomethings may feel at a loss when adulthood suddenly overtakes them. I've seen people in their late twenties quite surprised and shocked when they realize their peers at work are just high school students, and they are working dead-end jobs at high school wages. This realization can trigger a feeling of depression or inadequacy. I have seen grown twentysomethings with their heads bowed in tears, wondering what's next and wondering why others are passing them by.

That's a wake-up call, a call to action, to take advantage of that sweet spot described above by Dr. Jay. The choice of acting versus not acting appears to simplify the problem by only providing two options: 1) loaf around and feel guilty for wasting away your twenties, and 2) complying to a rigid and society approved career and social path.

If I am given a choice of two tracks, compliance or loafing, I will jump the tracks, break free, and forge my own path without a GPS device blindly calculating my destination. When our children were small, we would occasionally spend a day in San Francisco, California with a rule to bring no maps. GPS was not available back then. We went without maps for the excitement of making discoveries we wouldn't have otherwise found. On that peninsula you always knew the directions north, south, east, and west, so you would never be truly lost. The experience was enriched by the path we chose. The path in life is the experience.

I'm not opposed to maps. They have their place. When I travel cross-country, maps provide me a broad picture of where I am and gives me an infinity of options for where I can go. You cannot experience that with a GPS app that performs its unseen calculations somewhere outside of your vision.

Success is not a fad or a myth. It is a choice, followed by action and more choices along your path. Whether or not a leap of faith is a success or a flop, lessons are learned and skills improved. Failures are painful, but they are foundations for success. Wins and losses ultimately add up to what it means to be truly successful. Making decisions and following through requires not only imagination but also a lot of courage. That route on a fixed track is so much easier, but it is not of your own making. Creating your own success is tough. In today's world, making choices can be one of the most difficult things we have to face.

It's even harder when others are openly critical of your hopes, dreams, and goals. It can be lonely for a time. For those who act and exercise courage, the third decade of life provides multiple chances for successful and fulfilling ventures. To determine where you want to be, you need to be aware of both the opportunities and the challenges of your place and time. Twenty-five is the midpoint of this important decade and commonly thought of as the age when our brains are fully developed, and our bodies are commonly thought of as being in their prime.[21]

Finding success and modeling your life now and in the future is not limited to twentysomethings. We will see examples

---

21   *TED,* "Meg Jay: Why 30 Is Not the New 20," May 13, 2013, video, 14:49.

here and in future chapters of teenagers and older people who have found the inspiration to apply the benefits generally understood to belong to twentysomethings. As a twentysomething, you have greater freedom to make mistakes. Though you may get looked down on, this gives you a pass. People almost expect you to flounder at times.

Brian Parker is a twenty-nine-year-old medical student and an entrepreneur. I met him in a lobby of the campus student center when he was a young undergrad student. He was anxious to tell me he was starting a successful charity called Limitless. He raised funds through various 5K runs and other activities. He donated the proceeds to diabetes research. Bullied as a child, Brian chose to take things in stride and develop a nature to learn from experience and to always be aware of people, their circumstances, and their needs.

He wanted to make a difference, not just go to class and follow a routine. He remembers a specific day when he was fasting and praying to find some new opportunity. He felt in his heart there was something he needed to do. Then he saw a girl he knew from church. She was praying for the same thing and looking for someone to help her. He learned she was diabetic. Then he brought in his friend Connor to build the Limitless charity for diabetes awareness and research.

Sometime later I remember how excited Brian was to unveil a Kickstarter campaign to market a unique travel pillow which he called the Morph Pillow. That turned out to be one of those experiences you build on. In his own words, "That was a fun project. It was a horrible failure. I'll tell you what, when you hear about businesspeople and failed projects and stuff, it's a real thing. I just had no idea what I was doing. I made errors in terms of how much I was paying out of pocket for the product, among other things."

Recently I saw him, and he said he had just come from a franchise sales meeting. I was surprised when he told me it was for his retail fireworks company. I thought, "This is one energetic twentysomething." He is the owner. Fireworks? That was new to me. He then told me about his close fortysomething friend, Duncan Lillico. They were fellow entrepreneurs, each working their own ventures, the twentysomething and the fortysomething each encouraging the other.

While networking in local entrepreneur groups and meeting other people, he became friends with Duncan Lillico. Duncan was working a regular job while also running a property development company. He also started the Provo Fireworks Company with an innovative online presence to go along with the traditional tent sales. In the state of Utah, fireworks can only be sold during dates specified by the state around specific holidays: Independence Day, Pioneer Day, New Year's Eve, and Chinese New Year. The company was doing well when the unexpected happened.

On November 21, 2018, at age forty-two, Duncan suddenly died of a pulmonary embolism. He left behind a wife and three children. Along with his family, the Provo Fireworks Company was in limbo. Brian had heard about his friend's death. Then he noticed Duncan's wife had posted on her Facebook page she wanted to sell the fireworks company. Time passed and Brian noticed the company was still for sale. He was not in a position to buy the company himself, but he told her he was looking for a buyer among his associates.

The window for the next holiday, Independence Day, was approaching. With no potential buyers, Brian offered to conduct a fire sale of the existing inventory. Time was short. Brian went to work to get everything set up for the sale that would occur on a Thursday, Friday, and Saturday. Brian and Duncan's widow agreed on an 80/20 split of the liquidation proceeds, with Brian getting 20 percent. The sale was a huge success, and he cut her a check for her portion, which was $65,000. His portion turned out to be like a good summer job for him, helping him pay for medical school.

The story did not end there. After the sale, they were packing up and Brian asked her what she was going to do with the company now that the sale was over. She told him she could let it dissolve. Then she made him an offer. She said she was sure Duncan would have wanted Brian to take over the company. She considered his efforts and the earnings of the liquidation sale as payment in full for the company.

To honor Duncan, he changed the name of the company to Duncan's Fireworks, with 10 percent of all profits still going to the Lillico family. Brian now has seasonal work to help support him through medical school. His experience shows the potential versatility of people in their twenties, quickly adapting to new circumstances and recognizing opportunities to make a difference.

The lessons learned are more valuable than if everything had gone smoothly. *Psychology Today* says, "To fail is deeply human; everyone, no matter their background, skill set, or life story will fail spectacularly at least once in their life... But learning to be okay with making mistakes, big or small, is a critical skill—one tied not only to resilience but also, perhaps, to future success."[22] About his failed pillow venture, Brian concluded, "It is okay. Well, I've never heard of a millionaire out there who didn't have a company they lost money on, you know, and so it's just kind of par for the course and I learned a lot, a whole lot."

I have worked with twentysomethings during most of my life. I started as a teenager, working on campus at Utah State University. I worked as a custodian in student housing and as a groundskeeper. I got to work with student employees and be around college students. My next experience around twentysomethings was when I lived that decade myself.

I was up on a ladder when I first met Demetrios on a construction project. One of my professors at college grabbed a bunch of students, including myself, to help speed up the project and give it a burst of energy. Demetrios was the owner of the new venture, a retail nursery store. He immigrated to the United States to further his studies. He specializes in developing and marketing garden seeds for crops in colder environments with a short growing season.

I stayed on working at the nursery when it opened. It was a great job for a twentysomething in college. Studying horticulture made me a perfect fit to effectively sell and give

---

22 Psychology Today Basics, "What Creates Resilience," *Psychology Today*, September 7, 2020.

professional advice. He was a great example of driving your dream forward. His business evolved to become Mountain Valley Seed Company and True Leaf Market.[23]

As with my other jobs during that time in my life, I was working mostly with other people in their twenties. I often thought about what good employees they were. Most were hardworking and quick to learn. They had goals in life; they saw working in a small business as a steppingstone, a learning opportunity for their future.

After my graduation in 1981, I moved to California. But the nursery industry nationwide was in a slump. To survive, I worked as a security guard at the San Onofre nuclear power plant for a short time. I was assigned to sit on top of a fourteen-foot ladder and watch for oceangoing intruders. It was pretty at first, but it just made me seasick after a few hours. I was looking through barbed wire fencing with the ocean moving behind it. I only lasted two weeks. It was a lonely job, but important since security cameras weren't yet standard fixtures. In my two weeks, I encountered no intruders.

My lifelong plans were more than on hold, they seemed to be evaporating because of the economy. I learned the world was constantly changing, and to survive you can do most anything for a time while searching for and setting a new course.

The COVID-19 experience, starting in 2020, is another example of how quickly circumstances and opportunities

---

23   True Leaf Market, "About Demetrios Agathangelides"," accessed January 27, 2021.

can change. Some of my favorite ethnic restaurants did not survive the pandemic. The Thai-Ger was one of them. The owner almost closed the restaurant when a business partner pulled out in 2019. He regrouped and recovered. Then in early 2020 he had a stroke, and his faithful employees kept the restaurant going. One of his twentysomethings stepped up to lead them through that challenging time.

Recovering from his stroke, he was back to work for good, or so he thought. When the pandemic hit in March 2020, the state prohibited dine-in options. The Thai-Ger fought back with a takeout menu and sold cloth face masks on the side. It wasn't enough. On May 7, 2020, a posting on Facebook said the business was temporarily closed. A June 16, 2020 post said they were permanently closed.[24]

Utah Restaurant Association president and CEO Melva Sine said by September 2020, nearly 10 percent of Utah restaurants had closed due to the pandemic. She said that represents at least 452 closures. She said the challenge now is to regain consumer confidence. Restaurants are averaging operations at only 35–40 percent capacity.[25] These statistics are less alarming when compared to other areas that have been hit harder.

A survey by the New York State Restaurant Association taken at the end of August 2020 showed only 36.4 percent of restaurants in the survey reported being "likely or somewhat likely"

---

24   Thai-Ger's Facebook Page, accessed January 27, 2021.

25   Graham Dudley, "Nearly 10% of Utah Restaurants Have Closed for Good, Association Says," *KSL News,* September 2, 2020.

to stay open and serve customers for the foreseeable future.[26] Each closure affects owners, investors, landlords, customers, and communities at large. The individual and collective stories of resilience and triumph through innovation will surface.

Adapting to circumstances requires reassessment and redirection as it relates to your life's trajectory and desires in life. The adaptability of young people to leverage new circumstances amazes me. My friend Brandon Owens was working a job where sales were flat during the pandemic. With COVID-19, some markets slowed down, while others increased. He was concerned about his future in sales. Working remotely became so standard that he was recruited online for his new job in a growing market. His new job is working with software for home education, with increased demand as a result of the pandemic. Brandon is working for a company in another state. He has never met his boss face to face and is now in the process of assisting to hire other employees, which he may never meet in person.

By age twenty-seven, I had a small family to support. Although I had to maneuver a sluggish economy, I did what I could until I found a new career path. I was searching for something I had been preparing for, without even realizing it. I was working as a commercial air conditioning mechanic in Silicon Valley. It was a great opportunity in many ways, and I loved my employer and my crew.

However, I had a powerful feeling there was something else I needed to be doing. After learning about and witnessing

---

26   Carlie Porterfield, "A Staggering 64% of New York Restaurants Could Shut for Good by 2021, Analysis Says"," *Forbes,* September 4, 2020.

police work via my friend Ron, I found myself gaining insight during my oral board interview to become a police officer. The probing questions actually helped me see how my experiences in life prepared me for this new career path. I personally experienced having to adapt and redirect more than a couple of times during my twenties.

Authors Brett and Kate McKay describe what they call the twentysomething brain advantage, which is "The passionate, uninhibited motivation to fearlessly go after your passions, figure out life's big questions, and make important commitments."[27] I had big questions. I was fortunate to never feel discouraged during that time. I was flexible and kept adapting as I searched.

In your twenties you have the benefits of youth and the capacity of an adult. Your mind and body are on the cusp of being fully developed and at their peak performance and resilience. You have enough life experience to rally in your successes and to overcome failure. You've overcome challenges, and you're likely working through challenges right now. To a greater or lesser degree, you have also likely experienced and learned from some form of trauma in your life.

You have freedom. A twentysomething is typically not tied down to a mortgage or a high-paying job, both of which could limit your mobility. If you have a family, your young children are still adaptable to change. Since you're just starting out, you are resilient to any kind of change.

---

27 Brett McKay and Kate McKacy, "Don't Waste Your Twenties Part I: Taking Advantage of the Unique Powers of the Twentysomething Brain," *A Man's Life,* accessed August 21, 2020.

You have a lot to be grateful for. It's easy and sometimes tempting to cast blame at circumstances and perhaps give up or, as they say, throw in the towel. While working on police patrol, I met a young man I'll call Michael. He was approaching his twenties but was struggling through his later teen years. He had, from what I remember the old-timers calling, a chip on his shoulder. *Cambridge Dictionary* defines having a chip on your shoulder as "to seem angry" all the time because you think you have been treated unfairly or feel you are not as good as other people.[28]

Michael was definitely not feeling so great about himself. He appeared to also have a list of grievances, though we both opted not to go there. He was in a learning mode. I could see he was figuring out the importance of not dwelling on his complaints. He was also picking up on the futility of reliving his own mistakes. He wanted to move forward but was still carrying too much unnecessary baggage.

It was obvious he was really down. As a police officer, I have found we (police) often see people at their lowest points in life. Emotions can be overwhelming. He was stealing again, which was a recurring problem for him. Michael had developed an addiction to stealing and couldn't explain why he felt such a compulsion. Addiction to theft is a very real thing. I have seen it repeatedly. It most commonly surfaces in shoplifters who often steal things they don't even want or need. I've even seen very wealthy people shoplifting petty items just for the thrill of the theft. It's like a gambler at the roulette wheel,

---

28 Cambridge Dictionary, s.v. "have a chip on your shoulder," accessed January 13, 2021.

thrilled at the anticipation of losing. Though it may be hard to understand, the thrill of the risks can be powerful.

Psychologists Dr. Tony W. Buchanan of Saint Louis University and Dr. William R. Lovallo of the University of Oklahoma state that stress episodes can increase the propensity for addiction.[29] I've often seen a tendency for addictions to surface when people are under stress or feeling negative toward themselves. This was the case for Michael. Unfortunately, succumbing to the addiction does not create relief. It may only temporarily mask feelings or postpone misery. The only initial benefit to the addiction in this case is to draw attention to and help recognize deeper problems that need addressing.

This turned out to be a valuable moment, a chance to address negative experiences and choices and focus on the positive. Too often in life we focus so much on the negative and become so obsessed with it that it overshadows any good we may have. Michael was down on himself. He needed a lift. Deflecting from the negative, I suggested he look at the advantages he had in life and take stock of what he had going for him. He was feeling so bitter he couldn't think of anything. He said, "Like what?"

I asked if he had a home, a mom, and a dad. He was starting to feel a bit grateful as he answered in the affirmative. I pointed out some things he had accomplished and things he was in the process of overcoming. He was intelligent and was blessed with a good education. He was a good student. He

---

29 Tony W. Buchanan, and William R. Lovallo, "Abstract: The Role of Genetics in Stress Effects on Health and Addiction," *National Institute of Health, National Library of Medicine,* accessed January 27, 2021.

was good looking and likable. It was obvious others wanted to be around him.

I'm pretty sure I saw tears forming as he said, "Nobody ever told me any of those things before." As Michael recognized he had good things going for him, it reinforced in my mind the importance of seeking gratitude. He really did have a lot going for him; the list kept building as he thought more about it.

Like Michael, you can assess what you've got going for you. Here are some attributes to consider:

- Freedom

  - Twentysomethings can change jobs or job location. They can more easily pick up stakes and move on.

  - As we get older, we are more tied to careers, benefit plans, community, children's schools, mortgages, and more.

- Mental and physical development

  - It is generally understood the major development of the brain is complete by age twenty-five, while the body is in its prime.

  - Though brain development is slower past age thirty, we can still exercise our mental capacity, maintain and expand human interaction, and challenge ourselves to new ideas, ventures, and other experiences.

- Courage and faith

  - It is easier for younger people to walk by blind faith and bounce back from setbacks.

  - People past their twenties have had more experiences of being let down or disappointed by other people or changes of circumstances.

- Experience

  - By the time most people reach their twenties, they've had some successes as well as failures to build upon, even though they may still be more idealistic and less fearful of future failures.

  - As we get older, we see and experience more pitfalls and may be more inclined to stereotype situations or people we meet.

- Mentor magnetism

  - People with more experience in life are frequently anxious to help. Many of them will practically stand in line to offer encouragement or advice to people younger than themselves. They've been there and want to share their valuable wisdom and experience. Good people want to see others succeed.

  - As people get older, attracting mentors is less spontaneous. Maybe others assume you've been there and you've got this. However, if your peers or younger people know you can use support, they will also learn to stand in line to help and advise. They also get the bonus of tapping into your knowledge and experience.

As Dr. Jay teaches us, to be in your twenties really is a sweet spot. It is a time of action. In this chapter we've seen the world is in motion and always changing. I first noticed this at age twenty-one when I returned from two years living in Chile. I spent all that time learning a foreign culture and coming home, I realized a lot can change while you're away. There were new buildings here, a rerouted highway there, and my favorite candy bars went up in price. As I tried to analyze my culture, I realized I had changed even more than the culture around me. I was in that sweet spot, a verified twentysomething, ready and willing to experience and learn. I was free to search out and build my own path.

This chapter shows how quickly twentysomethings can exercise their courage by adapting to change and bouncing back from adversity. We've also seen how older people—those over thirty—can work with twentysomethings to create success. This was seen with Duncan, who even after his death influenced a twentysomething to continue his work. Demetrios, the farmer and scientist, surrounded himself with twentysomethings to build his business. When the owner of the Thai-Ger restaurant had a stroke, one of his twentysomething employees stepped up to save the restaurant, at least for a time.

The following chapters will demonstrate how these and other benefits typically available to twentysomethings can be had at any age, though the obstacles may be different.

CHAPTER 2

FREEDOM IN YOUR TWENTIES

—

*"In a curious way, age is simpler than youth,
for it has so many fewer options."*

—STANLEY KUNITZ

Shockwaves and a loud sound of an explosion spread through much of a seven-story campus dormitory building. Mornings were typically pretty quiet when most residents were in class or sleeping in. Rather than shelter in place or run away from the blast, dozens of curious, mostly eighteen-year-old residents were drawn from the building to see what had happened.

The head resident, a mature adult who supervised the building, called the plumbing shop following the blast. Because of her quick investigation, she requested a replacement for a broken toilet in a communal restroom. The plumber said he would send somebody out to assess the damage and see if they could just replace the broken parts.

She assured him the toilet could not be repaired; it was shattered into hundreds of pieces. When he asked how the toilet broke, she told him a student had accidentally dropped a bowling ball in the toilet bowl when he stepped into the stall to use the toilet. The plumber said something like, "If you believe that lady, we need to talk."

A group of residents had gone to a second-hand thrift store for fun, to relieve some stress, not knowing what treasures would be waiting. Some bowling balls happened to be there that lucky day and drew the boys' interest. Their imaginations kicked into gear as they brought them back to the dorms, and the young scientists got to work. They played the "what would happen if" game. Testing questions like, "How high do you have to go to drop a bowling ball before it will break?" and, "When it breaks, does it split in two or shatter?" Probably not giving it much thought, they wondered how a bowling ball would do in a toilet.

One of them took aim, tossing the ball as if shooting a free throw for one-point. He made a perfect shot. The toilet blew in pieces, clearing the way for a direct hit onto the drainpipe. The impact reverberated through the drainpipes, shaking the entire building. It sounded like an explosion.

The first time moving away from home is an abrupt change. You finally get to make more of your own decisions. At the same time, the separation from home and family can be hard to overcome. Whether or not they admit it, feelings of loneliness can be very real. Though only one person tossed the bowling ball, it was a social event for building new connections. The bowling ball toss was more than a random event, it was an experience along the path of life during a time of discovery. None of the boys knew what a spectacular event that would turn out to be. Fortunately, no one was injured by flying chards of porcelain.

Was he punished? The developing adult who tossed the bowling ball paid the cost to purchase and install a shiny new fixture. He and his friends gained life experience, preparing them for further learning and growth through their twenties and beyond.

I've seen that in a group setting such experimentation is not uncommon among this age group. In a college setting, such experimentation creates distraction from the stresses of schoolwork and the loneliness we call homesickness.

Most of these young adults were technically children a few weeks or months before. Their brains are actively developing and stimulated to make connections based on experience. They're learning firsthand about cause and effect, good practice to get ready for their twenties.

Though we share many types of experiences, each of us as an individual works out our own path, adventures, and mishaps. The twentysomething experience with freedom may start with leaving home for the first time. This can happen as early as age seventeen, or in many cases may not actually happen until age thirty or later. Just like everyone else over thirty, I am a former twentysomething. I've been there. If you are a teenager now, you'll be a twentysomething soon.

When I was a cop in San Jose, California, San Jose State University was part of my police beat. I spent twenty-five years as a cop at Brigham Young University (BYU) at the foot of the mountains in Provo, Utah. I've learned a lot about people in their twenties. One of my charges as a campus cop was to maintain peace in the campus dorms. That's how I came to learn how much damage a bowling ball can do to a toilet.

Soon after I took the job, I determined I needed to meet and get to know any dorm residents who were still awake past 11:30 p.m. at night. By that time, most of them were too tired to study and too wound up to sleep. Behavioral excesses were a product of their age and their environment.

My role was to maintain the peace and a safe environment. Spending a great deal of time around them, I learned to earn their respect and confidence, becoming a supportive coach and mentor to help them understand cause and effect and the importance of decision making. They sensed a sort of security knowing the consequences of delinquent action and feeling those in authority really cared about their well-being. Some students told me they sometimes abandoned harmful pranks out of respect for me, not wanting to disappoint me.

They were learning, and their brains were developing, making new synaptic connections. Mental Health Daily reports, "When you're eighteen, you're roughly halfway through the entire stage of development. The prefrontal cortex doesn't have nearly the functional capacity at age eighteen as it does at twenty-five."[30]

---

30 "At What Age Is The Brain Fully Developed?," *Mental Health Daily,* accessed January 20, 2021.

I've seen incoming freshmen with a list of things they were going to do to express their much-anticipated freedom. Stories of college behavior and pranks are passed down from previous generations or are glorified in movie and television content and viewed as a rite of passage. Some of those lists included typical college pranks, such as throwing a burning Bart Simpson doll out of a seventh-floor window, launching water balloons at passers-by, or putting live chickens through the window into a dorm room.

They planned some pranks. Others were more spontaneous, often triggered by the stress of discovering college classes were much more demanding than high school courses.

Dr. Marty Nemko is a career and personal coach who recognizes twentysomethings who graduate from college still have new transitions and stresses to deal with. He asserts academically trained graduates often feel insecure jumping into a job search. He says they suffer from the fear of imposter syndrome.[31] The reality is you are never fully prepared for your next phase. If you're going to progress, you need to take on challenges beyond your current comfort zone.

You don't need permission to be an adult. Once you've completed your eighteenth year, you are one. Dr. Nemko suggests moving forward and learning as you go.

"Key to curing the imposter syndrome is to accept you are a beginner. Then maintain an experimental

---

31   Marty Nemko, "Curing Career Fear: Not-Magic Pills for Reducing Career Anxiety," *Psycology Today,* Jun 24, 2018.

mindset: Try things out and change when they don't work. Ask for candid feedback from clients, customers, and especially from master practitioners.[32]

I finished my undergraduate education in 1981, graduating from Utah State University in Logan, Utah. I followed the societal norms as I understood them. I got a job related to my BS in horticulture. I went to work in landscape maintenance for an Ohio company named Tru-Green. Despite a slow economy, business was booming in the Salt Lake City market where I worked. We were all in our twenties and worked our tails off in both sales and service. In recognition of our hard work and high productivity, the company rewarded us with a Las Vegas vacation. They presented each of us with a t-shirt with the declaration, "I survived Salt Lake City." With a big smile, Dan, our branch manager, proudly accepted his shirt that read, "I survived BECAUSE of Salt Lake City."

The company was also expanding an office in San Jose and looking for people to transfer. My wife and I each had roots in California and the pay was higher, so with a casual, fearless, twentysomething perspective and hardly any thought, we jumped at it. At that young age, there was nothing holding us back. It was another bright spot in the economy. With the growth of the high-tech industry in a burgeoning Silicon Valley, opportunities for commercial accounts abounded. The revenue generated per man hour was significantly higher on commercial accounts. For a company that covered mostly midwestern and mountain states, this new emphasis was novel.

---

32   Ibid.

Still in my twenties, everything was going well, and my career path was secure. There would soon be opportunities for advancement. I hadn't calculated the high rental rates. I didn't know my pay would not keep up with the higher cost of living in California. The company gave me a modest raise to compensate for the cost of living, but it didn't come close to making up the difference.

In my twenties, I didn't really think things through or make those calculations ahead of time. I had freedom. I naively assumed things would work out. I didn't yet fully grasp cause and effect. Was it courage or ignorance? If courage means overcoming fear, then it was ignorance. For me, that was a blessing. That naïve assumption led me to new paths and discoveries.

Things worked out somehow. At Tru-Green, I was going for a promotion I was highly qualified for—a regional horticulturist. I didn't get it. Unexpectedly, the job went to a nephew of a high-level executive who lived on the East Coast. His qualifications were lacking. They asked me to bring him up to par and train him.

That triggered my decision to move on, again without thinking too deeply about it. Whether or not things would have eventually worked out had I stayed, I'll never know. You cannot change a path you have already passed over, nor would you want to. Had I taken a different direction at any juncture, I would not be the person I am today. Every time you select a different path, your future reality changes.

I didn't know during this whole time, the groundwork for another opportunity was being laid in advance. It could be

God's way of answering prayers, to guide us where we might not have been looking.

My wife Jenny was traveling from the San Jose International Airport. While waiting at the gate, she met a stranger named Bill Thomas. He was excited to hear we were moving to San Jose, and even more so when he found out we would be neighbors and attend the same church.

Bill was looking to hire a new HVAC mechanic for his company. He came to our apartment and asked me what I knew about mechanical systems. I told him, "not much, but I have an aptitude for learning." That wasn't the answer I would recommend for an impromptu job interview. The job paid more than my job with Tru-Green, relieving a lot of stress. I changed my path solely based on financial need. It turned out to be a valuable experience.

With high-tech companies expanding throughout Silicon Valley, business was booming for air conditioning contractors. It was a great opportunity for twentysomethings, like myself, looking for a secure job with union benefits.

With his wisdom of experience, Bill Thomas found a unique niche in the market. He noticed with new building construction and remodel it was common for general contractors to save costs by skimping on air systems. The deficiencies were not immediately visible and were softened by the typical one-year warranty. When something went wrong, they would send someone out to fix the problem. At that one-year mark they would realize their systems couldn't perform adequately. In the high-tech industry, HVAC systems are critical. Failing cooling or air filtration systems can shut down production in a flash.

Bill would check city and county building permits that had been issued for HVAC a year and a half previously. He would call up and say, "How's your HVAC system?" As expected, frequently they would say they were frustrated, and their warranty had just expired. At that point, sales flowed in naturally as he explained how their systems were deficient and how his crew of mechanics could finally resolve the problems.

Based on my experience, it is easy to see how twentysomethings can be so indecisive, such as frequently changing jobs or changing majors in college. I had an inherent fear of commitment or being locked into something that closes off alternate paths. I was becoming a job hopper.

Penelope Trunk is the founder of Brazen Careerist, a social network for young professionals. She has run a career blog for over twenty years. In an article for *Associated Career Management Australia*, she said on average people in their twenties change jobs every eighteen months.[33]

According to Penelope, my job changes were normal. In my own quiet way, I was exerting the freedom of being a twentysomething. She says job hopping is good as long as you are gaining valuable experience and networking along the way. Trunk says thoughtful job hoppers have more job stability because they control how and when to change jobs rather than

---

33 Penelope Trunk, "Why Job Hoppers Do Well," *Associated Career Management Australia*, accessed September 27, 2020.

being susceptible to layoffs, downsizing, or reorganization. Surprisingly, she said job hoppers typically are more loyal because they bring outside experience to the table and quickly adapt to new teams. They bring with them experiences from multiple jobs with varying challenges.[34]

My oral board for the San Jose Police Department consisted of a city council member, police officers, a police sergeant, and community leaders. When they asked which job most prepared me to be a police officer, I thought through a variety of jobs and experiences. I didn't tell them about my security job on top of a ladder at a nuclear power plant; they might have laughed.

I told them about a job where I had to think on my feet and make quick decisions, recognize out of the ordinary events, work under stress, and overcome challenges. The board members were nodding in agreement. When I told them the job title, short-order cook, the nodding in agreement changed to a blank expression on their faces. I had to connect the dots for them. I explained how my experiences gave me highly transferable skills appropriate to police work.

In addition to the rigorous duties in a busy kitchen, I had to manage through product shortages due to food product distribution problems. An oil embargo and nationwide fuel shortages triggered the whole mess. The disruptions caused us to randomly change menu offerings as dictated by product availability. It also motivated my team and me to treat our suppliers with consideration, hoping to gain some favoritism.

---

34   Ibid.

The oil embargo was imposed by OPEC (Organization of Petroleum Exporting Countries). OPEC cut oil exports to countries that supported Israel during the Yom Kippur War of 1973.[35]

"At 10:00 p.m. on December 3, 1973, a thirty-seven-year-old trucker from Overland Park, Kansas named J.W. Edwards stopped his rig suddenly in the middle of Interstate 80 near Blakeslee, Pennsylvania."[36] He was almost out of fuel. Fuel rationing had made fuel impossible to obtain at truck stop after truck stop. At that point he expressed his frustration over CB (Citizens Band) radio and stopped his big rig, blocking the highway. Other drivers heard his rant and joined in the protest to block highways. Protests spread nationwide. The trucker protests led to one hundred thousand layoffs. My food shortages at my restaurant were just part of the ripple effect.[37]

During this time of shortages, filling orders was challenging for our suppliers. We had to think on our feet and to learn organizational and negotiating skills. John Rich, the boss, was a strong mentor to me. He always adapted and came up with solutions. Little did he know he was preparing me for a future police career. All these and more skills were very applicable to serving in law enforcement, as I saw firsthand when I later became a police officer. You have to think on your feet, quickly adapting to fast changing circumstances.

---

35 "OPEC Enacts Oil Embargo," *History,* accessed January 20, 2021.

36 Joseph A. Williams, "When Truckers Shut down America to Protest Oil Prices—and Became Folk Heroes," *History: History Stories,* updated January 15, 2019.

37 Ibid.

Building trusting relationships and negotiating are indispensable in police work.

Later in my career, I found my jobs in landscape maintenance and air conditioning prepared me to oversee security systems to create a safe environment. Just as in former jobs, I found myself on planning committees and working with management, plus a variety of contractors and suppliers. You are always gaining skills you can use in the future. As a police officer and security professional at BYU, I worked with mechanical and electrical tradesmen and engineers, architects, and contractors. I was already familiar with all those specialties. Job hopping in my twenties enriched my career path.

As Dr. Meg Jay learned, the importance of what you learn and what you do or don't do in your twenties impacts your entire life.[38] Every decision or indecision becomes a part of you and how you will impact your future world. It's a time of accelerated growth as you test your freedom and test out decisions. You don't have to pull pranks to become successful, but every experience teaches you something.

As you transition from your teens to your twenties, you typically don't have a mortgage or a job that locks you into a benefits package. If you don't have kids yet, you can travel the world. With few obligations and no permanent home, you might even take a job in Thailand, the Czech Republic, or anywhere else. You can change jobs on a whim or even go without a job for a while. Whatever you do, you will learn and carry that learning throughout your life.

---

38 *TED*, "Meg Jay: Why 30 Is Not the New 20," May 13, 2013. Video, 14:49.

Whether you're just waiting for something to happen or moving forward, it can be difficult. My wife and I attended a motivational talk addressed to young married couples. As the presenter spoke, he listed the challenges we were facing, balancing work, school, time with your spouse, and finances. He talked about that term paper due in a few days and who would watch the baby tomorrow and the price of diapers. I felt this thought in my heart, "This man understands me." I strongly suspect everyone in the room felt something similar. Then he talked about the relief we anticipated as we looked forward to graduation and truly getting out on our own. I could definitely relate to that.

Then he jolted us into a new reality, saying, "Life will only get harder!" I heard someone utter in complaint, "What!" You could hear sighs all around.

The speaker gave this reassurance, "But you will get better at it!" The decade of your twenties presents unlimited options and paths. He explained our twenties were preparing us for greater responsibilities ahead.

CHAPTER 3

SILICON VALLEY TWENTYSOMETHINGS

———

"Someone said, 'You Might Fail. And I say, so what's wrong with failing? The most important thing is to have more successes than failures."

—KEN OSHMAN

Santa Clara, California

ROLM Corporation, 4900 Old Ironsides Drive

Before the mobile phone era, ROLM Corporation dominated in the design and production of office phones and office phone systems.

As a commercial air conditioning mechanic in Silicon Valley around 1982 I got a work order for an air conditioning repair at a company called ROLM. I came in through a service entrance and soon realized there was something different about the facility. Then I realized something was different about the whole company. Like other businesses, there were parking lots, mechanical systems, offices, light switches, drinking fountains, and people. Those were things I normally take for granted. ROLM not only had a unique name, but the facility also had a unique environment.

The first difference that really stood out to me was how meticulously clean everything was, from floor to ceiling, even in the back corridors and utility rooms. I don't mean to say I hadn't seen other clean facilities, but this one topped the list. Other physical features stood out, such as a lap swimming pool and the indoor and outdoor fitness facilities. There were streams and ponds in a parklike setting. Having worked in both custodial and landscape services, I was impressed. To me, a clean and inviting facility says a lot about how the company is run. Though I was there on an air conditioning service call, the company immediately intrigued me.

As an air conditioning mechanic, I was the proverbial fly on the wall inside many high-tech facilities, including Apple and IBM. Donning a blue Dickies work uniform and a tool belt made me blend in, as an extension of the mechanical systems or another piece of furniture. People hardly noticed me, even when I had to work right in their workspaces. This company was different.

From 1968 to1969, four electrical engineers put together a business plan for a new company named ROLM. Though you may not recognize the name today, ROLM was a familiar name in office telephone systems well into the '90s. The company revolutionized office phone systems technology that had stagnated under AT&T for forty years. They also developed the first off-the-shelf ruggedized computers for military use under extreme conditions such as extremely high heat and cold. In less than twenty years, ROLM was a Fortune 500 company with over 659 million dollars in annual sales. They were competing with other Fortune 500 companies that were founded many decades before.

These engineers called the new company ROLM, using the first letter of each of their surnames: Gene Richeson, Ken Oshman, Walter Loewenstern, and Bob Maxfield. All the other names they thought of were taken by some other company. The name ROLM was temporary until they could come up with something else. Running the new business became a priority over renaming the company. So, the name stuck. They were all graduates of Rice University, a private research university in Houston, Texas.[39]

They were twentysomethings, except for Walter, who was barely thirty-two. Walter's interest as an electrical engineer was first inspired by his dad, who was an engineer in Germany until he was banned from working as an engineer because he was a Jew. Seeking freedom, he fled to the United States in 1929.

Walter found work at Sylvania, an early developer of light bulbs and vacuum tubes. On his own time, Walter started developing a product of his own. When he told his boss about it, he was given the option to drop the project or quit Sylvania. He quit on the spot, saying later:

---

39 *Computer History Museum,* "ROLM Corporation, Competing with Giants," May 19, 2004, video, 1:27:21.

*"The threat didn't frighten me—I had no assets to
lose, and there were abundant jobs for engineers."*[40]

He exercised his freedom to change paths even though he
didn't yet know what was next. He may not have had a plan,
but he knew he wanted to leave. Maybe it was an act of faith.
His father had fled Germany into the unknown because he
had run out of options. Walter left Sylvania assured there
would be options.

After he quit Sylvania (or was fired as others suspected), he
was in a poker game with Ken Oshman and other friends.
He casually mentioned he had just quit his job. Ken picked
up on it and called him the next day, proposing they start a
company. They brought Gene Richeson into the group.

Gene demonstrated an entrepreneurial spirit at age eleven
when he went into retail egg production. He bought a hundred baby chicks, raised them to maturity, then sold half of
them. The remaining fifty produced eggs, which he sold door
to door. He kept re-investing as he marketed and around his
hometown of Paris, Texas. At its peak, his farm had six hundred laying hens. He marketed and distributed his product
with a home delivery service, delivering the eggs early in the
morning before school. He exercised skills in farming, production, sales, and product distribution. His future potential
venture capitalists recognized the transferable skills he was

---

40 Katherine Maxfield, *Starting Up Silicon Valley: How ROLM Became
a Cultural Icon and a Fortune 500 Company* (Austin: Emerald Book
Company, 2014), 9.

developing at a young age. He bought a motor scooter with his profits, a definite win.[41]

Ken reached out to Bob Maxfield, a good pick considering he was the top student in his class at Rice. Ken trusted him so much that back when he was a grad assistant at Rice University, he used Bob's completed exams as answer keys to grade the exams of the other students. He definitely wanted him on the team and called to invite him to join the new start-up.

Bob was a dedicated student and competitive swimmer who set relentlessly high expectations for himself. Other swimmers on his high school team noticed how anxious he was, saying he was a nervous wreck before every swim meet. He expected a lot from himself and won races accordingly. His anxiety worked in his favor by giving him results. This trait was reinforced when he worked as a summer camp counselor. He taught water sports under the direction of Tex Robertson, a former Navy SEAL officer.[42] In her book *The Power of Different,* psychologist Gail Saltz says outside of actual anxiety disorders, the term anxiety is frequently used to describe a feeling that motivates you to perform at a high level and in some environments is considered a "badge of honor."[43] This characteristic explains his class ranking at Rice. His determination prepared him for channeling the kind of motivation it would take to run a start-up company from the ground up.

41 Katherine Maxfield, Starting Up Silicon Valley: How ROLM Became a Cultural Icon and a Fortune 500 Company (Austin: Emerald Book Company, 2014), 4-12.

42 Ibid.

43 Gail Saltz, The Power of Different: The Link Between Disorder and Genius (New York, Flatiron Books, 2017), 81.

There were many secure jobs with a regular paycheck for someone with Bob's qualifications. In a panel discussion with the ROLM founders in 2004, Bob described his shock when Ken invited him to join the start-up. "I got this feeling of sheer terror in my throat. I had several offers for good salaries, a four-month-old baby, and was living in a little two-bedroom apartment. So, I said sure, what the hell?"[44]

Gene, Ken, Walter, and Bob were all earning graduate degrees at Stanford University while working as electrical engineers at other companies such as Sylvania and IBM. Before he was even hired at Sylvania, Ken told his boss he was thinking about starting a company. He sensed his boss was not keen on the idea of him competing in the electronics industry. His boss, Burt McMurtry, asked what kind of company he would start. Ken deflected the focus and avoided a direct answer by saying, "I don't know. Might be a shoe factory."[45]

The four engineers brainstormed ideas and put together a business plan. They came up with a few product ideas, but with their lack of experience they had done no market research to see if the products were viable. They were engineers not formally trained in business. Then they sought capital, not an easy task for these young engineers just out of college. They approached seven different venture capital (VC) firms and were flatly rejected by all of them. Bob Maxfield explained:

---

44 *Computer History Museum*, "ROLM Corporation, Competing with Giants," May 19, 2004, video, 1:27:21.

45 Katherine Maxfield, Starting up Silicon Valley: How ROLM Became a Cultural Icon and a Fortune 500 Company (Austin: Emerald Book Company, 2014), 5.

*"We were all twentysomethings, all engineers,
no marketing guy, no finance background,
no manufacturing background."*[46]

One of the VC reps, Jack Melchor, told them they came in
with a jumble of product ideas and mismatched markets. He
told them their product ideas were junk.[47]

Jack couldn't recommend anyone risk money on such a weak
proposal by four men with little experience and no track
record. He really couldn't justify it, either. But he sensed
something beyond their lack of experience and preparation.
He saw raw potential on the talent and the drive of these
young engineers. Trusting his feelings, he coached them and
helped them build a solid business plan. They discarded all
their ideas and took a step back. Gene came up with the idea
to fill a void in the market he picked up on at a recent trade
show. They would make ruggedized off-the-shelf computers
for the military.

Military in-flight computers were expensive and custom
made, one at a time. Try to imagine a flight computer with
a unique, one-of-a-kind operating system with no compat-
ibility with other flight computers. The opposite of that is
described as by the term "off-the-shelf," meaning one that is
not customized but can be purchased from stock on hand.[48]

---

46 Computer History Museum, "ROLM Corporation, Competing with
   Giants," May 19, 2004, video, 1:27:21.

47 Katherine Maxfield, Starting up Silicon Valley: How ROLM Became
   a Cultural Icon and a Fortune 500 Company (Austin: Emerald Book
   Company, 2014), 15.

48 *Merriam-Webster*, s.v. "off-the-shelf," accessed February 5, 2021.

If they could produce it, they could sell it at a fraction of the cost of the custom units.

These twentysomething engineers were going to build computers, but they needed software and an operating system. This concept was an emerging trend in the industry. To put it in context, this was years before the PC Windows, MacIntosh, and Linux operating systems, even more than a decade before MS-DOS. The timing was perfect because of the need for a lower cost solution and because another new startup company, Data General, provided the base system they needed. Data General started building microcomputers in 1968. The owner of the new company, Edson de Castro, was eager to work a deal for technology with the ROLM team. From 1968 on, Data General became a leader in fast microcomputers until they were bought out by EMC Corporation in 1999.[49]

They still needed capital. As the goals came together with a viable product filling a viable market, Jack gained more confidence. But he felt they needed a greater commitment. He offered to put in $15,000 of his own money if each of the four would also pony up the same amount. That was no small amount in 1969; it was the cost of a nice house. They all agreed and found the money, mostly borrowing from parents, grandparents, and other relatives. Working with Jack, they determined $75,000 was still short of what they needed to develop, manufacture, and market their new product. Their own commitment to the venture was enough to convince the

---

49 *Computer History Museum,* "ROLM Corporation, Competing with Giants," May 19, 2004, video, 1:27:21.

Bank of America to grant $100,000 in credit, bringing their startup capital total to $175,000.[50]

Jack was supportive of helping secure future venture capital after the team committed to two milestones: 1) Produce a prototype computer before the Joint Computer Conference, which was eight months away, and 2) Receive orders as a result of the trade show. If they didn't meet the milestones, they would certainly fold. There would be no second chance.

They rented an old prune drying shed for eighty-five dollars a month, and no air conditioning, as an office. Most suppliers, upon seeing their meager office, demanded cash payment for everything. They were up and running.

They met their goals. They produced a prototype computer in eight months and received product orders at the trade show. That was just the beginning of their challenges and successes. Within only fifteen years, they were listed as a Fortune 500 company.[51]

After several years, new challenges appeared. The military customers were threatening to force them to share their designs with other companies who would compete against them. Somehow, through the bureaucracy of the military, a rule surfaced requiring contract suppliers must produce multiple

50 Katherine Maxfield, *Starting up Silicon Valley: How ROLM Became a Cultural Icon and a Fortune 500 Company* (Austin: Emerald Book Company, 2014), 20-24.

51 Katherine Maxfield, *Starting up Silicon Valley: How ROLM Became a Cultural Icon and a Fortune 500 Company* (Austin: Emerald Book Company, 2014), 236.

distinct products to qualify as vendors. ROLM would need to come up with additional products. Additionally, the market for the military computers was becoming saturated.

A new opportunity came up. For decades, AT&T had a monopoly on phone systems and equipment. That was about to change. Until November 1968, no user of the nationwide telephone network could connect non-AT&T equipment to the network. That meant businesses could not set up their own telephone exchange and connect it to the outside world.

A new law, known as the Carterfone Law, for the first time allowed companies to tie their own equipment into the AT&T nationwide network. Thomas Carter, a manager of Texas oil fields, sued to challenge AT&T's monopoly over telephone equipment. He saw a need for better communication in the oil fields of Texas. He invented a phone that could patch into radio communications. His invention would connect oil bosses across the state, but only if the FCC would allow connecting equipment to the existing phone network.[52]

The Carter decision opened the phone network up, not just to Carter, but to a variety of new technologies. ROLM jumped in on the action and created a new product—a fully digitized and computerized phone system for businesses. The new CBX (Computerized Branch Exchange) replaced AT&T's PBX (Public Branch Exchange) that had seen no significant upgrades in forty years. The product was about to go nationwide. Digital hardware and software products were lab tested,

52 Matthew Lasar, "Any Lawful Device: Revisiting Carterfone on the Eve of the Net Neutrality Vote," *Ars Technica,* December 13, 2017.

then they were "beta" tested, typically by an outside firm. Often, a product end user would conduct a beta test by actually installing and using the product in the field.

ROLM engineers and managers took the risk of testing it on the ROLM Corporation campus. There were a lot of fears it might not perform up to standard. But they took the chance, confident they could trouble shoot any malfunctions. The first test was to rip out the AT&T equipment at the ROLM offices. One executive, Leo Chamberlain, said it wasn't ready or good enough to call the test a beta test, so he jokingly called it an "alpha" test.

The initial test was chaotic. The phones were programmed to chime when they detected an error. There were so many chimes that many employees wrapped their office phones in a jacket and stuffed them in a drawer to muffle the constant chiming. Chamberlain joked with all those chimes, some people actually started going back to church.[53]

Their success created another challenge: employee turnover. Engineers and developers were always on the watch for new and higher paying opportunities. The competition to hire and retain the best high-tech talent kept people moving from one company to another. Not only did this slow the work down, but it also increased the risk of losing knowledge to other companies. The transformation of the work environment that followed resulted in what I saw when I visited the company for a maintenance call.

---

53 *Computer History Museum,* "ROLM Corporation, Competing with Giants," May 19, 2004, video, 1:27:21.

Taking on the challenge of employee retention, ROLM management looked around the valley and found Hewlett-Packard had created a work environment that stimulated creativity and loyalty. They doubled down on the concept. They hired someone, a little older than them, to put a plan into action. That was Leo Chamberlain, an engineer himself. "At forty-four, I was about ten years older than anyone else at ROLM. I figured I was hired because the company needed a seasoned manager, someone with gray hair. I was so grateful to have such a fun, interesting job compared to the drudgery of my previous job that I sent Ken a humorous thank you note every week for the first two months."[54]

Leo became general manager and created what he called GPW—"Great Place to Work." With Leo's leadership, they established a management style that challenged each employee to high productivity and accountability. The company gave ample support, but limited micromanaging. They had full trust in their people.

This internal company history created the unique environment I had noticed. What I observed was in stark contrast to the stuffy industrial and office buildings I usually visited. There was something soothing and invigorating about the movement of the ebb and flow of people interacting with and moving through the environment. It reminded me of the feeling you get from the movement of distant ocean waves or the calming flames of a fireplace. Certainly, a great deal of thought and expense went into these facilities and the management and leadership that led to it.[55]

---

54 Ibid.

55 Ibid.

I saw various activities going on, people meeting outdoors, eating at tables, exercising, swimming, people moving from place to place, and even meditating. Labs and other workspaces had windows looking out onto the grounds that brought them together with the whole environment. Instead of access control systems, there were decorative pools, a trout-stocked brook, and a landscape to guide people where they needed to be. The cafeteria served up gourmet food at low prices, subsidized by the company.

The first person I met on my service call was a custodian sweeping a hallway. He welcomed me cheerfully. I asked how he liked his job. He stood up straight and said, "It's the best job I ever had, I love it here!" He told me about his role in maintaining an environment where the company could thrive.

Intrigued, I challenged him and asked if he knew who the CEO was. He said, "Sure! I had lunch with him yesterday." As my jaw dropped, he eased my awkwardness and explained how this executive enjoyed eating in the cafeteria with different employees every day. I don't remember the name the employee gave, but the general manager, Leo Chamberlain, regularly ate with a variety of employees.

IBM bought ROLM in 1984 and promised to keep the culture. I was very familiar with the atmosphere at IBM, as I usually spent at least a couple of days a week working in their facilities. I was in charge of air filtration for their entire campus. With my experience inside IBM, I didn't believe their top-down management style could long tolerate the open and interactive ROLM culture. Had they called me, I would have told them so. Four years later, IBM sold the name and technology to Siemens.[56] The facility was abandoned and fell victim to disrepair and vandalism.

What ROLM left behind was the inspiration and perseverance of four hopeful and courageous engineers. Thousands of ROLM employees took the ROLM culture and ingenuity with them as they started their own companies or went to work for other companies throughout Silicon Valley and throughout the world. If the company you work for has a relaxed interactive environment, subsidized or no-cost food service, state-of-the-art fitness facilities, and a management style that encourages problem solving at the lowest levels, somewhere through history your company might have been influenced by the "Great Place to Work" culture of ROLM.

Most current managers and employees probably do not know what ROLM was. Now, because of the impact of the COVID-19 pandemic, many engineers and other employees are currently working from home. Long-term impacts are yet to be seen. Though the names of these four engineers are not household names today, the impact of these twentysomethings will probably continue in some form. The quality of ROLM products was so solid that some ROLM telephone systems are still in use after more than thirty years.

These young entrepreneurs Gene, Ken, Walter, and Bob showed great courage to assert their freedom to move forward. They created a must-succeed formula. Once committed,

---

56   Katherine Maxfield, *Starting up Silicon Valley: How ROLM Became a Cultural Icon and a Fortune 500 Company* (Austin: Emerald Book Company, 2014), 241–269.

it would be very difficult to back out. They employed the following incentives:

- Hold yourselves accountable to trusted mentors.

- Adhere to research, development, production, and sales goals.

- Invest a sizable amount of your own money.

- Hold yourselves accountable to one another.

As the company grew, they earned employee loyalty by creating a rich environment where they wanted to thrive, produce, and market quality innovative products.

CHAPTER 4

TEEN FREEDOM

"The way we spend our time defines who we are."

—JONATHAN ESTRIN

Everyone over the age of twenty-nine was a developing twentysomething on a journey leading to today. Every twentysomething was once a developing teenager, and before that they were a child. My grandmother Aline spoke of the importance of building relationships and teaching children from the time they were born. She believed if a child was loved unselfishly and taught properly then they were basically fully raised somewhere around the age of seven to nine. As they reach their teenage years and exercise more and more freedom, they'll want to come to their parents for love, support, and advice.

The freedom of a teenager comes in degrees. There are a lot of changes and differences between a thirteen-year-old and a nineteen-year-old. They are the same person, but rapidly changing physically, intellectually, emotionally, and spiritually. Throughout teenage life you must ask for a ride because you don't have a driver's license. The upside to this is it creates an opportunity to spend more time one-on-one time with a parent, or an older, and hopefully wiser, sibling.

Dr. Susan McHale of Penn State University, distinguished professor of human development and family studies, and her colleagues show us that it's a common tendency for adolescents to spend time with parents. Spending time together gives youths the opportunity to receive validation and support.

"The stereotype that teenagers spend all their time holed up in their rooms or hanging out with friends is, indeed, just a stereotype."

—PENN STATE[57]

Though the teen era only lasts seven years, you gain a lot of freedom moving from age thirteen to nineteen. Unless you find yourself a caregiver for a relative, you have free time. Beyond school, you still have time for athletics, music, dance, skateboarding, snowboarding, shooting hoops, volunteering at a rescue center, or any of the other numerous options. Creating your own opportunities is another option. You may not realize it, but you probably have the most freedom you will ever have in life.

You have the potential to be fearless and idealistic. If you have a good support team, you may not consider failure a big deal. You've got plenty of time to start again or change

---

57 Penn State, "Time with parents is important for teens' well-being," *Science Daily,* August 21, 2012, accessed February 17, 2021.

your goals. You can find a job. Even a low-paying job gives you spending cash of your own, which you can learn to manage yourself.

But things are not always so ideal. The Pew Research Center reports seven in ten teens see anxiety and depression as major problems among their peers.[58]

These are serious issues, but they don't have to be. Dr. Marilyn Price-Mitchell of *Psychology Today* said, "From a research perspective, the data is clear that the seeds of healthy development are sown through the relationships that young people share with caring adults."[59]

John works side by side with his dad restoring old cars. He is a high school junior in rural Virginia and drives to school in a 1953 Ford he and his dad restored together. It just might be the shiniest car in the county. The engine hums along perfectly with a nostalgic sound to people who lived in an earlier time. He and his car must be the envy of a lot of older men as they hear a familiar sound coming down the road and look up to see this sixteen-year-old behind the wheel, smiling from ear to ear as he listens to tunes from the sixties. Working on and restoring old cars is such a big part of John's life that he doesn't remember the first time he picked up a wrench in his dad's garage. The passion has never stopped.

---

58 Juliana Menasce Horowitz and Nikki Graf, "Most U.S. Teens See Anxiety and Depression as a Major Problem Among Their Peers," Pew Research Center, February 20, 2019.

59 Marilyn Price-Mitchell, "Anxiety in Teens: How You Can Help," *Psychology Today* (blog), November 30, 2019.

The standard question people ask such an ambitious teenager is, "What are you going to do?" Or to top that, they ask, "What are you going to be?" Once, I asked John about his career path. How could I resist? I felt I could learn something new from this highly motivated young man. I recognized he already is doing amazing things and impacting the world. You don't have to wait to be somebody, you already are.

Philosopher Alain de Botton suggests we can get too caught up in judging what other people are or what they are going to be. He calls it career snobbery and suggests it can damage our self-image.[60] I had an occasional but recurring dream of having a junior high school guidance counselor recommend I enroll in a class that might be titled Building My Self-Esteem. I attached a stigma to it and figured it would take a semester just to cope with the label of being cast into such a class. De Botton brings up a similar dilemma as he describes going to the self-help section of a bookshop. He groups the books into two categories. One category says you can do anything and excel to whatever level you want. The second category claims to teach you to overcome your low self-esteem.[61]

John hasn't read any so-called self-help books. I don't know if he's ever heard of them. He has received positive support from family and neighbors who help him with his own goals and choices. He restores old cars and rekindles the culture of the era in which they were built. His answer to me about

---

60 *TED,* "Alain de Botton: A Kinder, Gentler Philosophy of Success," July 28, 2009, video, 16:51.

61 Ibid.

his future career came without hesitation! He is going to be a police officer. With such a decisive answer, I asked what or who inspired him toward a law enforcement career. He confidently tells me it's something he's always known. It's in his heart to serve.

When you meet somebody so ambitious, you've got to wonder who his mentors might be. Undoubtedly, the first that comes to mind for him is his dad. They've always worked on projects together. He also looks up to and has a special bond with his brother Billy, eight years his senior, a twentysomething who is a wealth of wisdom and support. These relationships make it natural for John to interact with and work with other adults. His hobby of restoring old cars makes it easy to strike up a conversation.

John sometimes wishes he got to meet the mentor he admires most, his great-grandfather Johnny. John said in admiration and tribute, "Well, Johnny, he worked on old cars too, and had a junkyard. So, I'm named after him and do the stuff he loved to do." He's heard about him from his family. Grandpa Johnny also left a well-known reputation around town that John wants to emulate.

A few weeks ago, John and his dad came across a 1956 Mercury Custom mired in a junkyard. They felt they just had to save it. John considers the purchase price an adoption fee; the car becomes part of the family. It will have a new life. John says it fits in nicely among the other cars.

Referring to this car he and his dad pulled out of the mud, John said:

"This baby might look like a piece of junk to y'all. But y'all don't see this as I do. I look at this car and see what it could be or what it used to be. The stories this car holds, even though it looks like it has never been touched, is what I look for. When I buy a car, it's not about how fast it goes or how stylish it looks. I love the history behind them."

John sees people the same way, not just the people connected with the history of a car, but other people in his life, including those who have passed on like Grandpa Johnny. Driving to school in his 1953 Ford is a catalyst for connecting with people. He's not a showoff, but others are drawn to him and his work.

Since the '56 Mercury Custom arrived at his property, John's fan base and influence have grown even more. A number of John's friends are now coming to the garage to learn the many skills involved in restoring old cars and are learning to gain an appreciation for them. John wants to help them, especially those who don't have the financial resources or the facilities to learn his art. He is their mentor and cares about them. What he says about cars he could easily say about people. Whether he spells it out in words or not, I think his heart may be saying, "I look at this person and see what they could be or what they used to be and can be again."

John is a child of the sixties. He is a virtual time traveler. He brings his peers along with him to learn and prosper from the past. For his older friends, he brings the past to the present. He restores what they felt in their teens and twenties and refreshes their view of the world. John's never taken any of those self-esteem courses you might find on the internet. He's too busy learning, leading, and teaching.

Four years ago, I went jogging on the Jordan River Trail that connects the Salt Lake Valley with Utah Valley through a shallow gorge called the River Narrows. I had planned on running a different trail that day but felt directed to change my plans. The change in course turned out to be very fortunate for me. I left the empty parking lot and joined with the trail as it led me and looped around and down toward the river bottoms.

I literally stopped in my tracks as I saw this guy riding his dirt bike on a parallel trail through the sagebrush. The trail had led me to the perfect spot to watch the rider perform. You would never have known the other trail was there unless you climbed up out of the ravine. It was well worn and looked like it had been there for a hundred years. It had a lot of valued imperfections, dips, and jumps, perfect for a dirt bike.

I was so impressed by the skill of the rider, I stopped to watch. I was pleased when I saw him loop around and practice on the same trail over and over. I had a front row view of the action. I thought back to my childhood and going out on the desert with my family to watch my dad and his twin brother compete on dirt bikes. As the rider practiced on the same section of trail over and over, I could see he was honing his already well-developed skills. With each run, his performance improved as his moves showed more confidence in the terrain.

On his last pass, he gave me a wave of the hand and rode down to meet me. After watching a great performance, I had a VIP backstage pass. Hunter was excited to tell me he had just discovered this particular trail. Impressed and inspired by his skills and demeanor, I wanted to know more about his motivation and training. He had a great backstage presence and was eager to share. Like was the case with John, through his conversation it was apparent he was accustomed to interacting with adults and bringing the generations together. He spoke most appreciably of his parents. As he spoke, I sensed a spiritual element in the joy he found in developing his talents and finding passion. He really enjoyed getting positive praise and recognition. It seemed to motivate him even more.

I was surprised to learn he was the only one in his family interested in motorcycles. He had free time to find and develop his interests. His parents supported him and took an interest in his hobby. He started with bicycle racing. From a very young age, he got into BMX bicycle competition. The term BMX came into use in the mid-1970s. It stands for bicycle-moto-cross, with the word cross symbolized by an X.[62] He excitedly shared with me some details of those BMX competitions. As he was maturing in mind, body, and spirit, he became fascinated with moving on to the challenge of dirt bikes and motocross competitions.

He explained he got into motorcycles "with grades." I thought by "grades" he meant step by step.

"No, no, no." He corrected me and told me how he negotiated with his parents to get a small bike with an 80cc (cubic centimeter) engine if he would produce a 4.0 GPA grade card. As he practiced on his 80cc, he was also getting older, giving him more freedom to work odd jobs to raise the money for a bigger bike, accessories, and safety equipment to finally compete in motocross.

---

62 *Merriam-Webster*, s.v. "BMX," accessed February 11, 2021.

Hunter's next goal was to learn freestyle riding, which was highly technical, requiring a lot more physical strength to manage and manipulate the bike through the course than his small, young body provided. At fifteen and a half years old, he was not complaining that he was too small. He patiently prepared to optimize his opportunities along the way. His body was maturing as he continued to train and prepare. He began working out at the gym to build muscle as his body continued to develop.

Looking back, I ask myself, "Was he successful? Was he living his dream?" That encounter was four years ago. Wherever Hunter is today, he's now entering his twenties. I'm confident his expression of freedom as a teenager has prepared him for continued development and fulfillment. On that once in a lifetime day, at that point where two trails came together, Hunter taught me the joy of finding and creating freedom and fulfillment along the path.

Fulfillment is not a badge or an endpoint, but rather it is part of your transformation as you become who you want to be. It should be your companion now, and into the future. Referring to goals in companies as a reflection of personal progress, writer Jori Hamilton also recommends continual transformation for any business. "If you approach business transformation within your company as a means to accomplish a goal, once you've realized that goal, the need to change will end."[63] The same principle applies to you as an individual.

We don't reach a goal and say we have arrived, then stop. That's what led to the famous decline of Kodak when they

---

63 Jori Hamilton, "Why Business Transformation Is an Ongoing Strategy and Not an Endpoint," *Best Techie,* accessed February 11, 2021.

invented the digital camera and decided not to produce or market it. The choice to stand still while competitors moved forward led to bankruptcy in 2012.[64]

Oliver W. Dahl is a twentysomething college student who just released a second collection of his photography in a bound book format. He tells me how much he loves the freedom of creating photographs while recording historic towns and buildings. But his publishing career started years ago. He loved to read juvenile fiction as a child and took on the challenge of writing in the genre he loved to read. Oliver had the creativity and the free time to write. He self-published his first book, *The Dreamers*, at age thirteen. He had the time and freedom to do something he wanted to do.

The book got terrible reviews because of grammatical errors and typos. He used the public comments to continue to refine the book through several editions, soon receiving a number of awards. By the time he was out of high school, he had created a sequel, *Nightmarers,* and another book entitled *Lies: Ann Putnam Jr.'s Recounting of the Salem Witch Trials.* Now in his twenties, Oliver continues his creative work. In addition to his photograph books, *Between Places,* and *Arco,* he's also working on his fourth fiction novel. Oliver's not standing still. He's living a full life in his twenties.[65]

John, Hunter, and Oliver imagined what they wanted to become and continue to push forward.

---

64 Chunka Mui, "How Kodak Failed," *Forbes,* January 18, 2012.

65 Oliver Dahl, "Oliver Dahl Homepage," accessed February 18, 2021.

John found inspiration in the lives of his dad, his older brother, and his grandpa. His accomplishments and generous heart bring him joy and satisfaction as people of all ages are drawn into his life. As a teenager, he has a greater understanding of all generations than anyone I know. That reaches beyond the grave. I'm grateful for his friendship and his positive influence in my life. As a bonus, he loves to listen to the music I grew up with.

Hunter was inspired by BMX bicycles. His family backed and supported him because they saw his determination. As he achieved his goals, he saw more and more opportunities and kept raising his goals. He prepared for his future developing adolescent body to compete at a higher level as he got older.

As a child, Oliver loved to read. Beyond his parents, his mentors were all of the authors he read. He combined the worlds he read about with his own imagination. With this foundation, he continues to create his world and build his future.

As you build your present into your future, think of who might inspire you or support you. You are free to become the person you want to be, and that begins now.

PART 2

MEET YOUR CHALLENGES

CHAPTER 5

CHANGE IS INEVITABLE

___

"A pessimist sees the difficulty in every opportunity; an optimist sees the opportunity in every difficulty."
—WINSTON CHURCHILL

There are pivotal times in world history. In March 2020 a virus, identified as COVID-19, spread throughout most of the world. Governments imposed a variety of restrictions, from closing various businesses to mandating people to stay home. Virtually everyone was impacted, directly or indirectly. Along with others, I hoped it would last a few weeks and we'd get back to "normal," back to a familiar routine.

As time went on, people began talking about how things would never be quite the same, how everyone would soon experience a "new normal." Dr. Lisa Maragakis, senior director of infection prevention at Johns Hopkins University, said, "The COVID-19 pandemic has changed life as we know it."[66]

___

66   Lisa Maragakis, "The New Normal and Coronavirus," *Johns Hopkins Medicine,* updated August 14, 2020, accessed September 21, 2020.

Though this pandemic is a driving force, it is not the only catalyst for change.

Change is inevitable. How you respond to change is up to you.

As the world changes, everything is evolving with it. Whether we choose to or not, we are constantly changing. We respond both spontaneously and deliberately. A brief encounter with a rattlesnake on a trail in the dark encouraged me to always keep my headlamp on when hiking at night, which is a permanent adaptation. Fortunately for my friend Baxter and me, the snake fled without attacking. In addition to individual circumstances, we are subject to the larger and more complex effects of a natural disaster, war, or political actions.

Hernán Aguayo was a clock repairman in the small town of Mulchén, Chile. In 1975, one of his customers paid his bill with a chicken instead of cash. It was hard to accumulate enough cash for any purchase because of outrageous hyperinflation. Bartering was a popular hedge against inflation. In this case, the customer just could not save up the cash to pay his bill. As fast as he saved, the cash lost its value as the monetary price for services kept going up. In 1975, the Chilean inflation rate ranged between 7.1 and 20.7 percent monthly. The average annual Chilean inflation rate for 1975 was over 340 percent.[67] This resulted from foreign and domestic policies and fluctuations in worldwide copper markets.

Hernán and his family lived in a beautiful home. The large chalet style house sat high on a slope overlooking the town

---

67 *World Inflation Data,* "Inflation Chile 1975," accessed February 9, 2021.

and river below. It stood apart from the typical adobe or stucco homes that were connected side by side, forming a perimeter around each city block.

I came to know Hernán when my missionary companion, John Lewis, and I arrived in town and were looking for a place to live. Before meeting him, we stayed a few days in a broken-down hotel. It didn't hit the star rating index. The water heater was broken. There were cat prints on the toilet seat. Water leaked onto the roll of toilet paper, and when we asked for new toilet paper, it took an entire day to get it. There was a general lack of typical amenities. Animals had full access to the inn, with a dog that enjoyed chasing a rooster down the hallway. The morning wake-up service was performed by the same rooster, right outside our door.

These adventurous living conditions became a driving force motivating us to find different accommodations. In Chile, the payment of room and board commonly provided living quarters in the home and meals together with the host family. In this small town, no such accommodations were advertised, so we would have to go door to door and see if someone would accept us into their home.

It was a short hike up the hill to an amazing chalet style house. We figured if we were going to search door to door to find a place to live, we might as well start with the nicest house in town. We introduced ourselves and made an offer for the first month, and future months depending upon inflation. Hernán Aguayo accepted our offer. But instead of a room, he rented out an entire wing of the house.

Besides owning and operating his clock repair shop, Hernán was always watching for business opportunities. He found ways to thrive, even though the country was suffering from extreme hyper-inflation. Bartering for goods or services was one of the adaptations to the economic conditions. His acceptance for learning and adapting is why he had a chicken in his backyard.

I had never seen a chicken slaughtered,
but that was about to change.

My reaction to the inflation was to learn fast. I had my monthly expenses sent from the US and converted to Chilean currency at a local bank. I quickly learned to spend, spend, spend, and never to hang onto local currency, even if it meant stocking up on toothpaste. I also learned to hold a few dollars in reserve, but didn't tell anybody.

In a feeble attempt to restore stability to their currency, the government made it illegal to trade or possess US dollars, except for US citizens. I don't know what the penalty would have been to sell dollars to locals, but I did not want to test it out. Despite the prohibition of trading in dollars, plenty of people asked if they could buy dollars from me. I could understand why. It was a frantic attempt to stabilize their own personal finances. Those were hard times.

Another effect of the inflation was mechanical computation machines didn't have enough zeros. The largest denomination of printed money was only 5,000 Chilean escudos, which at one time was worth about a dollar. Summer or winter I wore an overcoat to the bank to have enough pockets to accommodate my monthly withdrawal in local currency. For me, it was a minor inconvenience. For locals, the value of any money they might have saved quickly evaporated over and over again. To provide stability, the banks were storing wheat in large warehouses as a hedge against inflation.

Most people were paid their employment salary monthly, receiving a pay increase that more or less equaled inflation. The challenge was prices rose daily while wages rose only on payday. Many families would eat really well for two weeks after payday and practically starved the rest of the month. The money became so worthless so quickly that I once saw a man using a 100 escudo bill as a rag to check the oil on his car. The paper of the 100 escudo bill was notoriously soft and strong.

Rather than suffer or bemoaning his circumstance, Hernán continually adapted and adjusted to opportunities as they arose. In addition to bartering, he dealt with the inflation by astutely making the situation work to his advantage. He began trading in bicycles, scooters, motorcycles, and Jeeps. When Hernán shared his strategy with me, I became a teachable twentysomething, eager to learn from my fortysomething landlord.

This is how he explained to me the purchase and financing of his beautiful home in a time of hyper-inflation: he bought a bicycle. As soon as enough cash flowed in, he bought another bicycle, and eventually bought six bicycles. Meanwhile, these trading commodities were all appreciating in value against the currency. If you bought an item for 100,000 escudos, a month later you might sell the same item for 30 percent more, or 130,000 escudos.

He sold the six bicycles and bought a motor scooter, eventually six more bicycles and another motor scooter, and so on. By investing in these items, he overcame inflation. He continued to build wealth as he added other earnings to build up and resell his inventory. He continued to buy and sell bicycles, motor scooters, motorcycles, then Jeeps, and so on until he had the nicest house in town. An unexpected bonus came when we came along at just the right time to help maintain his cash flow with our monthly rent. Since our savings were in US dollars, our rent kept up with local inflation. After purchasing the house, he repeated the same process of buying bicycles and scooters and motorcycles until he was able to buy another Jeep to keep for his family.

The chicken he had taken in exchange for clock repair services ran freely in the yard. Other than the perimeter fence, the yard was no more equipped for housing chickens as the live-in housekeeper was to be slaughtering them for dinner. The eventful weekend came when the family went on vacation, traveling in a Jeep. Before they left, Hernán gave instructions to the housekeeper to fix the chicken in the yard for dinner. They told us the housekeeper would cook for us, though she did not know much about cooking. Hernán, with his dry sense of humor, gave us a wink and said, "Good luck." He must have laughed the entire weekend thinking about us, the housekeeper, and the chicken.

Then the time arrived for the chicken to be sacrificed. By the time she summoned us to the backyard, the housekeeper was already holding the chicken in one arm, stroking it as you would a family cat with the other hand. I was disappointed we missed the entertainment of her chasing and catching the chicken. I suspect apprehending and securing the chicken would have been well worth the price of admission.

She confessed she had never slaughtered a chicken and asked for advice. I told her my grandmother told me how her parents would cut the heads off with a hatchet and watch the headless animals run around the yard until they fell dead. She rejected that idea and described how she had seen it done by neighbors. While holding the chicken in one arm, she told me how they would stretch out the neck (her hands gestured as she spoke, actually pulling it by the head). She continued and said they would suddenly bend it and thrust downward, snapping the neck and instantly killing the animal. As she spoke, so it happened. In amazement she screamed out, "I did it!" She felt pretty accomplished, a win-win for everyone. We had chicken for dinner.

Unlike so many who struggled to stay afloat, Hernán was able to grasp and comprehend the bigger picture. Taking a proactive approach, he adapted so well he profited from the circumstances. Others either failed to see a bigger picture, or they chose to be victims.

If you were to spend time with police officers in a social setting, you would hear stories exchanged about real people dealing with real-life challenges. Many stories teach valuable lessons, such as how to be alert to potential danger. Other stories can deeply sadden you. Some stories make you laugh out loud when you realize everything turned out alright. All stories teach something about how to adapt to changing situations. There always seems to be at least one story so unique nobody else has experienced it.

While working as a San Jose police officer in the 1980s, I received a call reporting a shoplifter at a small mom-and-pop grocery store. The store owner described a man in his twenties or early thirties who had taken several quarts of Pennzoil motor oil off the shelf. The oil came in very recognizable bright yellow cans with the name Pennzoil emblazoned over an image of the US Liberty Bell. In thirty-three years of law enforcement, this was the only shoplifting case I encountered involving the theft of motor oil. The store owner reported the man fled on foot.

With a description of the suspect, I began searching through the neighborhood. He couldn't have gone too far carrying several quarts of oil.

Just a few blocks away, I saw a large old faded gray sedan on the side of the road with the hood up. A young mother and several children stood huddled together on the grass parkway watching their husband and father leaning over the car engine. Several bright yellow Pennzoil cans sat on the grass at their feet. Their gaze quickly shifted toward me as they saw my patrol car. By their appearance, it looked like they hadn't bathed or laundered their clothes in several days. The scene made me think of the Dust Bowl refugees as depicted in Steinbeck's *The Grapes of Wrath*, another story of people seeking a new normal amid harsh events or circumstances.[68]

I don't think the man saw me approach. I walked up as he was pouring a can of oil into the crankcase. He looked up at me and immediately confessed to the theft. He then shared

68   John Steinbeck, *The Grapes of Wrath* (New York: Viking Press, 1986).

a portion of his family's story. Finding work back home in the Midwest was tough. As the saying goes, they were down on their luck. Reading in the newspapers that the unemployment rate was lower in California and the economy was strong, they packed the car and ventured off, going on faith, not knowing beforehand what they would find or what they would do. To get into an apartment they would need first and last month's rent, plus a deposit, which was an impossible amount approaching $2,000 or more.

Their car developed a serious oil leak, and they were out of money. They'd been in town for a couple of weeks. Their problems got worse as he looked for even the most menial work. He was unbathed and unshaven as he had found nowhere to clean up or wash their clothes. The family's situation appeared hopeless, just like the Joad family from Steinbeck's novel, who were seeking work to survive.[69]

I went back to the little grocery store to report I had located and identified the thief working on his car as his young family looked on. I filled the store owner in on the family's story. With no hesitation, he said he would not press charges against the suspect.

Later that day, I was returning to the police station at the end of my shift and the route took me past that little store. As I drove by, I saw the suspect again. This time he was sweeping the parking lot at the store. I stopped to ask him what happened. After I left earlier that day, the store owner went and found him and his family. As soon as they met, the shopkeeper

---

69   Ibid.

felt a connection to this man. He hired him on the spot and helped the family make arrangements for their needs.

After hiring a man who had shoplifted from his store, I could imagine the fortysomething storeowner taking time to teach and mentor his new twentysomething employee much in the same way as my fortysomething Chilean landlord had mentored and taught me. I had learned so much more from Hernán than adapting and thriving during a period of hyper-inflation. Maintaining composure and entrepreneurship despite an awkward introduction put the storeowner in a position to mentor his new employee, as he wanted to learn to thrive in a new and challenging environment.

I've forgotten the name of this father and have had no contact with him since that event over thirty years ago. In my mind, I cannot refer to him as a thief, certainly not in the same way as typical shoplifters who are plagued with an addiction to steal.

This family acted spontaneously to their circumstances in the Midwest when they headed to California. It would be easy to say they were at rock bottom. Though desperate at that moment, they were adapting to their circumstance. With a job, they got enough of a reprieve to start making choices and building a new life. The parents were twentysomethings who launched into action without knowing how things would play out. They had courage to overcome fear and act to free themselves from a bad situation. Things were getting worse, but suddenly turned around when the store owner became both their first contact and first friend in California. Hope had arrived.

When I met Hernán, he was thriving in a harsh economy. I never thought to ask him what experiences he had as a teenager or a twentysomething that prepared him. Somewhere along his path he had learned to embrace change and overcome adversity. Maybe at some time he had been destitute or lived through trials or traumatic events. When I arrived in Chile, I was not aware that along with the inflation, Hernán's country had just been through a violent coup d'état which began on September 11, 1973, just over a year before my arrival.[70] People didn't talk about it. I don't know how he and his family might have been impacted by the coup.

I first recognized changes occurring when I moved to another country. I expected the environment to be different. My surprise was to return home and find that world had also changed. The destitute family and the wealthy clock shop owner recognized change and learned to adapt. Change is inevitable.

---

70 Ana Truesdale, "Memories of Chile's Coup D'éTat," *Chile Today,* September 12, 2019.

CHAPTER 6

MORE THAN A
SECOND CHANCE

———

*"As tough as it is to acknowledge, you had to go through
what you went through in order to get to where you
are today, and the evidence is that you did."*

—WAYNE DYER

Helen Lunney (Louise Hay) fled from Los Angeles to Chicago.[71] She had just given up her baby daughter for adoption
on her sixteenth birthday. Her childhood left her suffering
from physical and sexual trauma. Her environment had
failed her. Helen took a major step to find and create a new
environment. This was her second chance, but by no means
was it her only second chance.

When I took the final exam for the Utah Police Academy, I
only had two chances to pass. Fortunately, I passed on my

———

71   IMDB, "Louise Hay Biography," accessed April 7, 2021.

first attempt. I didn't need a second chance. In reality, if I failed my first and my second chance, I actually could have gone back further upstream and started the academy from scratch—a fresh start.

The concept of a second chance is not finite. During my police career, I've seen people emerge from a second chance and another second chance, over and over again. We don't talk about a second, then a third, a fourth, and so on. As we're learning and progressing throughout our life, the tally sheet is most likely listing the number of chances or choices as infinite. As we receive a second chance, we are given the opportunity to start again. It is not the end of the road. Redemption is not a one-time offer.

No matter the circumstances, you have choices. You can seek to change or improve your environment or change how you manage your circumstances. Viktor Frankl's observations during his experiences in a Nazi concentration camp led him to teach the importance of freedom of choice.

"The last of the human freedoms: to choose one's attitude in any given set of circumstances, to choose one's own way."
—VIKTOR FRANKL[72]

Helen's second chance in Chicago freed her from her traumatic childhood environment, but it did not yet free her from the trauma itself. Several years would pass before that would

---

72 Viktor E. Frankl, "Viktor E. Frankl Quote," Goodreads, accessed March 19, 2021.

happen. As a teenager, she worked a few low paying menial jobs in Chicago as she became a twentysomething.

In 1950 at twenty-four, she was at another fork in the road. She opted to take another chance and started over again, this time in New York. She even changed her name from Helen to Louise. She worked as a fashion model for Bill Blass and other designers. In her twenties, she went from working menial jobs to a successful career. Four years later, still in her twenties, she married a successful British businessman, Andrew Hay, and for fifteen years they had a good life. They traveled the world and mingled with people of high society. She had stuffed away her childhood and early teen trauma. She thought she had it made.[73]

The deep childhood trauma all came rushing back to the surface following another tremendous blow. Her husband Andrew left her for another woman. Louise was hurting. Dealing with the pain of a lifetime was a substantial burden. She had moved beyond her childhood traumas, but they resurfaced. She hadn't yet found healing.[74]

Looking for answers to deal with the current and past traumas, Louise began studying with the First Church of Religious Science, founded by Ernest Holmes in 1926. She learned about taking care of the mind and body through affirmations and other techniques. The experience was so beneficial in healing from her trauma that she got trained

---

73 Mark Oppenheimer, "The Queen of the New Age," *The New York Times Magazine*, May 4, 2008.

74 Louise Hay, "About," accessed March 11, 2021.

and became a Church of Religious Science practitioner. This was good preparation for her next trauma—cervical cancer. She declined medical treatments, following natural and metaphysical techniques she had learned. She felt to heal she needed to overcome her resentment for her childhood and learn to forgive.[75]

Author Benjamin Hardy, one of my great mentors, lived his teenage years in a stressful and often negative environment following the divorce of his parents. He speaks of a paradigm shift regarding his relationship with his father. "It used to be about how my father had failed me and my brothers."[76] As Ben lived through more experiences in his own life, his understanding of his father increased. His father has evolved over the years and so has Ben. Life's bumps create trauma. Whether major or minor, there is always room for healing and creating new second chances.

Louise was learning to heal from her traumas and illness and was teaching others to heal. She wrote a pamphlet in 1976 and a bestselling book in 1984.[77] She self-published a book and then opened a publishing house named Hay House. It was very rocky at first until she found the right person to sort things out. She hired an accountant by the name of Reid Tracy. He was not only an accountant to get the business organized, but he also became a valuable mentor.

---

75 Ibid.

76 Benjamin Hardy, *Personality Isn't Permanent: Break Free from Self-Limiting Beliefs and Rewrite Your Own Story* (New York: Portfolio, 2020), 159.

77 Louise Hay, *You Can Heal Your Life* (Carlsbad: Hay House, 1984).

Reid took the lead as CEO. The right person with the right motivation and talent was there when she needed him. Hay House became established and currently represents one hundred thirty authors teaching forms of self-discovery and self-improvement. The book *You Can Heal Your Life* became one of the highest selling books of all time, having sold over fifty million copies. Just past age sixty, Louise's new career took off. She was firmly established and so was Hay House. She passed away in 2017 at the age of ninety, leaving a thriving legacy.[78]

The life of Burgess Owens is a life of second chances. When he entered his twenties, he was in a sweet spot heading toward great success. He was studying at the University of Miami. As a twentysomething, he was a college football star earning many honors, including Superbowl Champion.

At age sixty-nine, he was still finding his twenty-five by fearlessly taking on new challenges. He was elected to the US Congress and began serving in January 2021. One of his campaign slogans was, "Our great nation of second chances." He shared his life history on his campaign web page.[79] I got to know him and his history even better at a campaign rally on September 21, 2020.[80] Even before his bid for congress, he was a sought-after motivational speaker.

78   Ibid.

79   Burgess Owens, "Resume-Bio," *Burgess 4 Utah,* accessed September 21, 2020.

80   Burgess Owens, "Live Campaign Rally," Talons Cove Golf Club, Saratoga Springs, Utah, September 21, 2020.

The earliest story of second chances he knew of in his family began in the hull of a slave ship.[81] His great-great grandfather, Silas Burgess, came to America when he was eight years old. He was sold on the auction block. He may have been a young teen when some men invited him to escape with them. Though risky, this was Grandpa Silas' second chance, a chance at a new start, a chance to break free from the shackles of slavery. They were assisted by members of the Underground Railroad.[82]

Silas established his freedom in Texas by working, saving, and prospering. He bought one hundred two acres of farmland and paid it off in two years. As he continued to thrive, he wanted to give opportunities to others, so he built a church and an elementary school for the community.[83]

At the campaign rally, I met Silas' great-great-grandson Burgess Owens. I learned he grew up in Tallahassee under Jim Crow, keeping the black and white populations separate. Despite the circumstances, he said he learned from his family upbringing that in America you can find your dreams. He teaches that there are always opportunities for immigrants. Burgess says no matter what circumstances you are in when you arrive in the United States, within a generation you can find great success.[84]

---

81 *News 19 WLTX*, "Burgess Owens speaks at RNC," August 26, 2020, video, 3:33.

82 Russell Contreras, "Story of the Underground Railroad to Mexico Gains Attention," *AP News*, September 12, 2020.

83 *News 19 WLTX*, "Burgess Owens speaks at RNC"," August 26, 2020, video, 3:33.

84 Burgess Owens, "Live Campaign Rally," Talons Cove Golf Club, Saratoga Springs, Utah, September 21, 2020.

While Burgess was growing up across the nation from me under Jim Crow laws in Tallahassee, I was in Los Angeles completely unaware segregationist laws still existed in the south. The movie *Remember the Titans* portrays a Virginia high school football team in 1971 where players were learning to overcome racial barriers within their team. There is a character named Ronnie "Sunshine" Bass who had recently arrived from California. I was also in high school at that time in history. I could easily relate to what he felt as neither of us had any idea segregation still existed.[85]

Burgess had his own connection to the movie. He lived it. He was one of four African American players integrated onto a football team at a white high school. Burgess said, "It was a rough year. It was similar to what happened in the movie, *Remember the Titans,* That was pretty much my experience."[86] Just like in the movie, once his high school team got past their racial issues, they got a second chance and started winning games.[87] This lead again to becoming a part of history and overcoming barriers, being the third African American to ever to receive a scholarship at the University of Miami.

After graduating and experiencing a successful college football career, the New York Jets recruited him. He and his team had seven losing seasons. Later he got the chance to play for the Oakland Raiders. The highlight of his NFL career was when, as underdogs, they won the Superbowl in 1980 against the

---

85   IMDB, "Remember the Titans," accessed March 19, 2021.

86   Trent Toone, "Former Oakland Raider Recounts LDS Conversion," *Deseret News*, May 30, 2013.

87   Ibid.

Philadelphia Eagles.[88] Burgess' football career dominated his third decade of life, his twenties.

Before retiring from the NFL at age thirty-two, Burgess planned ahead to by starting a business that would set him up for what he considered to be his life's mission to change the downward trajectory of his childhood community.

The decade of his thirties brought him down. He experienced two failed businesses, filing for bankruptcy twice. He suffered more setbacks, including prostate cancer and a divorce. He describes a difficult summer working as a chimney sweep by day and as a security guard at night while his family squeezed into a tiny basement apartment. It took him years to get himself back to middle class, working in the corporate world for twenty-five years.[89]

He talks about his long financial recovery, saying, "It was during these difficult chapters where life's most important lessons were learned."[90]

At the campaign rally he said, "I can now look back. This is what's great about aging, you can look back and see the journey, can see those times. Man, I really wish I wasn't there, but if you're like me, that was what helped you become who you are."[91]

---

88 *Fandom Pro/College American Football Wiki,* "Superbowl XV," accessed March 19, 2021.

89 *News 19 WLTX,* "Burgess Owens speaks at RNC"," August 26, 2020, video, 3:33.

90 Burgess Owens, "Resume-Bio," *Burgess 4 Utah,* accessed September 21, 2020.

91 Burgess Owens, "Live Campaign Rally," Talons Cove Golf Club, Saratoga Springs, Utah, September 21, 2020.

Finding success in your twenties trains you and gives you the confidence to overcome any future challenges and to find fulfillment in serving and lifting others.

Louise and Burgess each had their own genuine challenges in their teens. Both found success in their twenties, followed by serious challenges and setbacks. Another thing they had in common as the decades of their lives advanced was their motivation to build around service. Louise influenced innumerable people and that influence continues after her passing. Burgess is now serving troubled youth and a nation.

Whatever challenges you face or have faced in your teens or twenties are to prepare you for today and your future. Finding your twenty-five is discovering the doors to success remain open despite any hardships or failures.

CHAPTER 7

BACK IN THE GAME FOR YOUTH

———

"It's about who you've lifted up, who you've made better."
—DENZEL WASHINGTON

While I was in the police academy, an instructor issued the challenge to spend an ample amount of patrol time on foot and out of the patrol cruiser. Police officers are assigned to work a certain area during a specified time or shift. This is known as a police beat, and traditionally police would walk the beat. They would prevent and solve crimes by knowing the people who lived, worked, and visited the area. They would know when something was amiss because they knew the area. With the expansion of two-way radios, police beats could cover larger areas. The drawback was there was less direct contact with the people in the beat.

Saint Louis Police Chief Eugene Camp was getting complaints when he went to public meetings at the beginning of the 1970s. Every time he went to community meetings or met with local business leaders he was asked to restore foot patrol to the neighborhoods. Like many police departments across the country, the Saint Louis Police Department all but abandoned foot patrols during the 1950s.

The department ran a pilot program. The goal was to give the citizens a sense of safety and security. There were no expectations of preventing assaults or catching murderers in high-rise apartments. Chief Camp said, "Rather, we aim at heightened visibility of the police to reassure a scared public."[92] The surprising result was a 17 percent decrease in crime during the first five months of the program. Officers caught suspects in the act of committing crimes and directly prevented crimes such as saving a girl as her boyfriend was about to shoot her. Restaurant owners and other small businesses reported increased business.

Some people called and others wrote letters to thank the department for creating a safer environment. Some callers said they yanked their kids onto the street "to introduce them to a real, live police officer."[93]

I accepted the challenge of my academy instructor to be that real, live police officer. The opportunities he spoke of were the very reasons I was inspired to become a cop. As I worked my first beat in west San Jose, California, I got to know the shopkeepers, parks and recreation leaders, high school administrators and teachers, and many local residents.

92   "Law Enforcement: Walking the Beat," *Time*, December 18, 1972.

93   Ibid.

I expanded my knowledge and understanding of the community by visiting the high schools. I was invited to give police-community relations presentations. I was dedicated to learning more about what made some teens successful, and more about what some people call troubled teens. I wanted to better understand the young people I was hired to serve.

I appreciated the complexity of the challenges affecting teenagers. By just listening to these kids, I found some had become disinterested or lost hope. Many were open to or even sought the support of role models who understood and were willing to listen to them.

Working in a local high school as a substitute teacher provided additional experience interacting with and mentoring teenagers. I learned small things matter a lot when you're trying to establish who you are. I once made the mistake of teasing a student for what I thought was a goofy shirt. I didn't realize my teasing had impacted the student and promptly forgot all about it. Another student took me aside and told me the shirt I referred to was that student's favorite shirt, a key part of his identity. He wore it at least three times a week until I made a comment. He hadn't worn it since.

I don't remember the shirt or the comment I made, but it was a great lesson to me to seek understanding. I never saw that student again, but I prayed somehow some other connection would get him past my error. From that I learned to become a resource rather than a distraction. I came to know the needs, concerns, and challenges of a significant community of teens. They sought to deal with complex issues, looking to the future. I was determined to connect students with opportunities to thrive, reminding them continually to appreciate their potential and value.

As a substitute teacher, I learned some of the most restless or so-called rebellious students made really good teachers. Frequently, I would hand them a lesson plan and a piece of chalk and watch them quickly gain confidence.

Too often, the challenges of teenagers were trivialized by others and pushed aside as being of little consequence. In listening to them, I learned about real concerns adults sometimes ridiculed. I went through a training course on community-police relations. I was disappointed with one of our guest lecturers who had taught high school for over twenty years. He told us to not worry about trying to understand high school students. In summary he said teenagers are no more than a pair of jeans filled with hormones and are not worth the trouble to understand or communicate with. I find it troubling to see the lives of teens trivialized when they could really use role models and mentors.

Last year I went to a motivation conference. In one workshop, someone asked the instructor how a certain concept would apply to teenagers. I quickly forgot about whatever the concept was but remembered what happened next. Someone responded by saying it wasn't worth it to figure out teenagers, that you should just wait until they got older. An attendee, Scott, was one of just a handful of teens at the event. The comment stunned him. He came and talked to me about it during the next break, hoping for validation from me. Scott could have taken that comment as reason to isolate himself. Instead, he staked his ground. He chose to reach out to others.

The challenges Scott was facing in his own life were very real. He took this experience of someone saying teens weren't worth trying to figure out as a challenge. He wanted to help others at his school to better understand themselves and give them more confidence. He reached out to high school students, posting a promise on his Facebook page of his commitment to others who struggle. Rather than wait for somebody to reach out to him, he reached out to others and formed a community of teenagers who would strive to understand the challenges of their peers.

Our community, environment, and culture influence each one of us. Yes, we make choices, but discovering a positive and stimulating catalyst for opportunity and success may be all but hopeless unless the right person intervenes. If someone is feeling trapped or discouraged, connecting with someone who can listen, understand, and provide strategies, hope, and optimism could be life changing.

You can be that person, the person who reaches out.

As a San Jose police officer, a high school administrator called me in frustration over one of his students who had a habit of losing control and disrupting school. I'll call him Brad. The administrator explained he had been to the home and talked to the mother, who said she was also perplexed that each of her sons had struggled at fifteen years old. The administrator asked if Brad might be willing to talk with a police officer friend of his. Brad had previously refused to see a counselor but would feel more comfortable talking to a cop. My observation has been that a lot of kids respond well because cops are trained to listen and to seek viewpoints from different people. Brad had previous encounters with cops and knew he could trust them to listen.

When I asked the mother for permission to talk to Brad, she told me how each of her sons was arrested for something by the time they were sixteen. She said she was frustrated and didn't know what to do. She encouraged me to visit with her son, but she was sure it wouldn't do any good. As I stepped into the room, she reiterated he refused to go to counseling.

As I visited with the young man, I saw patterns of a disrupted home environment. He was grateful to express himself in the hopes I would listen. Through tears, Brad told me he felt lost and alone. He didn't have a father and felt he couldn't talk to his mom. She was too busy entertaining men she invited into the house to sleep with her. He had nobody to talk to about his internal pain, so he expressed his frustration by acting out, mostly at school. Brad was craving some kind of support, but didn't really know what that meant or how to find it. He didn't know who to reach out to, or how. He didn't want to go to counseling because he saw it as punishment and figured he'd be chastised rather than understood. He saw a spark of hope having me with him, someone to talk to who understood him and who he could trust.

I later updated the school administrator so he could work with the young man with a greater level of understanding. When I left the house, I suggested to the mother she might consider going to counseling herself to better understand her son. She lashed out at me and said, "He won't go to counseling!" She wasn't ready to understand her son. I saw hope in the caring school administrator to find help for Brad. Once he understood Brad's story, he was prepared to advocate and find resources for Brad.

Over the years, I've seen many teens striving to make the best of getting caught in the juvenile rehabilitation system. There are many factors at work to keep them cycling unsuccessfully through again and again. Knowing how to support them and what to say is not that easy. Just one careless comment can lower their confidence and increase their chances of returning. They see a detention guard or someone else roll their eyes and say something like, "You'll be back in soon, haha." Something like that, in a very real sense, erases options. It's easy for an outsider to say it is just a matter of choices. It's much more complex and goes much deeper than someone on the outside would imagine.

As of 2019, San Mateo County, California was running a program called Project Change. It is a program for juvenile inmates to complete high school while they're still in custody. The program gives opportunities for inmates to earn their high school diplomas, motivating them to find interest and satisfaction in progressing day to day. Inmates who earned their diplomas but still had a year or more to complete their sentence were regressing because they felt they had no more goals to reach for. They were bored to tears. Other than gaining recognition, the high school diploma had no immediate benefit. After a moment of pride and a brief recognition ceremony, what then?[94]

The program had the added benefit that upon their release from incarceration, successful students could continue taking college courses and reunite with their professors. The

---

94 Vanessa Rancano, "A Path to College for Kids in Juvenile Detention","
    Cal Matters, August 28, 2019.

program and its well-selected professors facilitated a bridge to the future. It provided confidence, a network, and a head start to a different path.

Even with the network of college professors, juveniles fall into the challenge of loneliness. Even when free, it's very difficult to break into new social circles. When your comfort zone is populated by toxic social groups, it's very difficult to leave them. One successful student, Nick Jasso, describes how loneliness played against his fight for freedom. It was difficult, and he felt alone. Nick said, "After I started changing the way I live my life, the hardest part for me was just being like extremely lonely all the time." He continued, "I couldn't hang around people who were selling drugs, so I just had to be by myself, and it was hard because it was the people I grew up with, the people I was closest to."[95]

Years ago, before I had ever thought about pursuing a career in law enforcement, my young friend David got into a juvenile detention camp that gave him opportunities to learn patterns of success and survival. It is my chosen nature to reach out when life is hard, so I went to see David at a juvenile detention camp. I ended up doing additional volunteer work there for other inmates, mostly one-on-one mentoring. David was quite excited about the structure of the program and how he was learning to thrive. He sold me on the concept and was proud of his progress and accomplishments.

David described how the camp was structured to provide opportunities for success and confidence building. He was

---

95 Ibid.

genuinely proud to share his progress as he earned points that rewarded him with privileges. The personal feeling of progress felt more important than the privileges. He was very proud to share his progress. He wore different colored belt loops representing his newly earned privileges. The boys liked to brag and high-five each other as they earned the belt loops and privileges. They had validation and recognition.

The highest privilege other than being released was the privilege to work, to perform physical labor. This included shovel and grounds work and various kitchen and janitorial duties. Work, or the ability to accomplish something, was definitely preferred. Boredom is punishing and creates a sensation of being hopelessly stuck and isolated. The work lifted their self-image, which increased their chances of success once released. A juvenile detention officer once explained it to me. He said when youth inmates come into the system, they are generally completely out of poker chips and feel like they're out of the game, the game of life. If you help them with a few chips and teach them how to earn more, they can get back in the game.

Seeking a career in law enforcement fit well with my inclination to reach out to people during difficult times. Holding onto David's story helped lift me when I would hear the stories of so many others who felt trapped in the system, not sensing there was any hope. My goal as a police officer was to open the door and let the light shine in.

Amid bureaucratic requirements, barely meeting the requirements on paper is too often considered good enough. Juveniles told me stories of how they would receive "packets" to replace school and be able to earn a diploma. Doing the packets meant filling in workbooks and hand-copying handouts without being challenged to search, create, or contribute. Every juvenile I've talked to who's been in the system described the packets as boring and tedious. The main goal was simply to maintain order in the facility, rather than preparing them for a productive future.

Former juvenile inmate Kent M. said, "They gave us handouts and told us to copy them. That was our schoolwork. I graduated from high school in Juvenile Hall, but I didn't learn anything in school there. I believe in the power of education. I read a lot of books on my own time while I was incarcerated. We never read a book together to discuss in class. I know they do that in high school but not in Juvenile Hall." They found an opportunity in having access to books.

At first, they were just a relief from boredom. Books became a key to opening the first door out of the trap of delinquency into new possibilities and freedom. He later went to college and landed a job as a policy analyst with a local chamber of commerce.[96]

Kent saw an out, a way out of boredom. He made a choice to read. He could read about other people. Whether real or fictitious, he got to experience the characters in books making choices, taking action, and overcoming challenges. In overcoming his boredom, he gained a connection with

---

96 Youth Law Center, "Educational Injustice: Barriers to Achievement and Higher Education for Youth in California Juvenile Court Schools," accessed February 12, 2021.

the world beyond the walls and fences of juvenile detention. More importantly, he gained a connection with a future.

GETTING INTO THE GAME

If your surroundings are holding you back, it's time to get back in the game. Whatever your age, you are in the prime of your life. You have what it takes.

Earlier in this chapter you met Brad. His circumstances at home were depressing. His mom brushed him off as worthless, certainly not worth her time or interest. It seemed natural for him to lash out in anger. I had a rare opportunity to interview Brad. I got to hear what he had to say and to feel what he felt.

I listened as he told me his mother was not likely to change her sad life anytime soon. In three short years he would graduate from high school and have the freedom to go out on his own. He couldn't change his circumstance, but he could change himself. He could no longer hide behind his situation. It was time to muster the courage to overcome his bitterness and fear and become the man he wanted to be, and to share that hope with others.

Like San Mateo County's Project Change and David's work camp, similar programs and organizations continue to spring up across the nation. Before being elected to Congress, Burgess Owens started a program called Second Chance 4 Youth. Maurice Eagan is the program director and says the organization wants "to give those kids that are stuck in state detention centers a chance to live a life that they can be proud of." Maurice is grateful for his second chance, and he said,

"Growing up as a kid in East Oakland, I was surrounded by, you know, alcoholics, drug addicts, pimps, and prostitutes. No surprise I became an alcoholic and a drug addict myself. It turned around for me after getting arrested again, facing new charges." He found a program that helped him find himself in time for adulthood and now wants to share that hope.[97]

Being free is difficult, but it's worth it. It takes effort. Once you sense freedom, you realize it's time to pay it forward. On the contrary, it's easy to think about all the things that hold you back. When you push through your fears, you start to see a glimmer of hope. The more you push forward, the brighter that glimmer becomes. There is no greater feeling than fulfilling your potential as you serve others

97   Maurice Eagan, *Second Chance 4 Youth*, "Second Chance 4 Youth-The Vision"," December 28, 2020, video, 4:13.

CHAPTER 8

LESSONS FROM BIPOLAR DISORDER AND ADDICTION

"I don't like people who have never fallen or stumbled."

—BORIS PASTERNAK

Dr. Konstantine Berejkoff, a Russian physician, escaped from the Soviet Union to the United States.[98] The details handed down by word of mouth are very limited. His grandson, Nicholas Berejkoff, shared with me some of the few things he is aware of. During or after the Russian Revolution (1917–1923), Konstantine fled east via the Trans-Siberian Railway, then across China. Nicholas' grandparents mentioned before sailing to San Francisco, Konstantine lived among a substantial population of Russian refugees in what they described as the

---

98 *Lake County Record Bee,* "Obituary George Berejkoff," May 8, 2008.

"Paris of the East," near Shanghai.[99] While working in China, he met and married Paraskovia Lamochkina, a Russian nurse who was also a refugee.

As his family struggled through piecing together clues about the history of Konstantine and Paraskovia, Nicholas felt a strong connection to his Russian heritage and his surname. He enjoys Russian food and culture. I asked him how he decided on Russian names for his four children. "I don't know that I necessarily ever had a moment where I wanted to give all my kids Russian names. It was always just there; giving them any names that weren't Russian just never even occurred to me."

Nicholas is deeply curious about the type of trials and struggles Konstantine must have had while escaping from the Soviet Union, then living as a refugee in China, and later as an immigrant to the United States. All Nicholas really knows about Konstantine's life is he had lived in a military school starting at around age eight to ten years old, and later he became a doctor. Nicholas cannot understand why his grandfather shied away from family activities. It was difficult to talk to him. Nicholas feels he must have suffered a great deal of trauma he never felt he was able to talk about. Konstantine married about eight times before finally settling in with one wife for the last fifteen years of his life.

Although Nicholas barely had a relationship with his grandfather, he was determined to be empathetic and avoid negative

---

99   Kristin Baird Rattini, "A Short History of Shanghai," *New York Times Archives,* accessed February 13, 2021.

thoughts or harsh judgment. He said, "He (Konstantine) went through very difficult experiences we can't really comprehend—immigration and being a refugee and all those kinds of things. I mean, look at how blessed we are. Look at how we were raised and the way we grew up. I don't know what it's like to be a refugee and go to war, or for soldiers to march you out of town in the middle of winter with no home to go to. Yeah, I don't know any of those things."

Nicholas tells me continually how blessed he is, yet he has faced and still faces significant challenges of his own. As he recalled, it started in his teens and early twenties. He was hurting and didn't know why. As young as the age of fourteen, he contemplated suicide, or as he calls it, "going back home." Though he was, and still is, unceasingly grateful for his parents and every opportunity they gave him to succeed, something was wrong. He felt like a stranger in his own life and in this world.

At age eighteen he took his first drink of alcohol and he recalled, "I was addicted the very first time I ever tried it. It completely overtook and overcame my entire world and took control." He laments falling into the alcohol trap, saying it can be so hard as a teenager to fathom the consequences of even one small decision.

He told me, "If I could go back to eighteen-year-old Nick, I'd say, 'Hey, this is going to destroy your life. For many times over, it's going to destroy relationships, it's going to destroy careers, it's going to just destroy your spirituality, and it's going to wreak so much havoc on your life.' You couldn't possibly understand. You couldn't."

About a year after his first drink, on a sober day, he suffered greatly from someone else's drinking. But he calls it his own big mistake. He got into a car driven by a friend who had been drinking. Nicholas knew he shouldn't ride with him, but the social pressure from his other friends was too strong, and he got in the car with them and they subsequently got in a serious accident.

As a result of the crash, he broke his back, and his body and organs were torn apart. He had many follow-up surgeries and was put in a body cast as part of his complex treatment. He suffered what he calls an incredible amount of pain, both physically and emotionally. His organs and other parts eventually recovered, though he still suffers from a lot of back pain.

Though he suffered, Nicholas always sought spiritual comfort and direction. He said there are two kinds of people when life gets hard, those who fall on their knees and turn to God and those who turn away and blame him.

He was in the hospital for a long time, which kept him sheltered from alcohol. He saw it as an opportunity to break from his addiction to alcohol and gave it up, or so he thought. It didn't last. Something deeper was going on. Maybe the alcohol was an escape from the pain he had experienced since he was a teenager, that same pain that tempted him toward suicide. He felt he had a good support network, including family and a few key friends. But he felt uneasy; things were still not right. He needed a change of environment, a fresh start.

That spiritual part prompted him to make a move. Rather than stew over it, he acted.

At age twenty, he threw a bag of clothes and a couple items important to him into his pickup. He spoke with his parents and told them he was leaving, then drove away. After hearing a friend had moved to Utah, he followed suit. He was looking for peace and direction. He wanted freedom, but from what exactly, he wasn't sure. Actually, he didn't know. Something was wrong.

The move was far tougher than he thought. The loneliness of not knowing anyone was overwhelming.

He landed in an apartment complex filled with college students. Seeking spiritual comfort and guidance, he attended church with these twentysomethings. That's how I met him; I was a volunteer leader in his congregation. He set a goal to volunteer as a full-time church missionary, which included abstaining from alcohol. This was more than a change of environment; it was a two-year commitment. He dedicated himself and served in the northeastern United States, mostly in Maine. He thrived in the structured and spiritual environment, surrounded by others his own age to mentor and be mentored by. He also had older leaders to teach and mentor him. Though thriving, Nicholas still had underlying challenges which surfaced again once he returned home.

As a teenager, he had wondered why he was so miserable. He described himself as often being in hell and reaching for a hand to pull him out. He figured somewhere along the way there must be a reason for his suffering. There must be something to learn or gain from all that misery. He continued to search to understand it, yet it continued. In addition to his work as a missionary, he continued to serve. Though he was suffering, he didn't want to play the role of a victim. He wanted to help others. "I thought of people who were sick in an outward way. You know, I thought of blind people or people with cancer or people who were homeless. I knew people had problems I didn't have. So, I figured this was the problem I have that they don't have."

I recently asked to meet with Nicholas to learn more about how he is managing things, despite continuing to confront challenges. He said he needed some time to prepare his mind. Nicholas explained he had laid out his life in his mind in a panoramic view so he could talk to me and refer to that picture. I'm impressed he takes notes in his mind which stay there for days or longer and that he can modify from time to time, like I might move post-it notes around on a whiteboard. If he is going to give a public presentation in church or the community, he writes his talk in his mind. He can go back to those notes and even make modifications.

I had only heard of a description of such a mental panoramic view from one other person. My friend Josh described a similar use of his mind with great detail. But, like Nicholas, he felt something was wrong. In his twenties, Josh decided to see a counselor. He was diagnosed with bipolar disorder. He didn't know why he had tremendous swings of hyper-activity and painful depression, or why he sometimes felt suicidal. These together with a number of other potential symptoms are often key indicators of bipolar disorder.[100]

---

100 Annamarya Scaccia, "How to Recognize and Treat Bipolar Disorder in Teens," *Healthline,* accessed March 29, 2021.

When Josh explained this phenomenon of a mental panoramic view, I recognized the same description as an indicator of bipolar disorder as described by psychiatrist Dr. Gail Saltz.[101] That was in addition to the symptoms he was already quite aware of. I mentioned to Josh I recognized his panoramic mental imagery as a characteristic of being bipolar. He was surprised it fell in line with other known characteristic of bipolar disorder. He assumed everyone's thoughts worked the same way.

I spent a lot of time with Josh while he was learning about his bipolar condition and how to manage it, mostly just because we were good friends, but also to support him in developing strategies. He realized while he was in a manic phase he had a compulsion to buy clothes. Binge shopping is another common symptom.[102] Having good taste in clothes, he was accumulating a sizable and high-quality wardrobe. But it was a burden to his overall budget. His solution was to make a choice ahead of time when he wasn't in an overexcited or manic state. He created a special budget for this. He put the budgeted amount of cash in an envelope for shopping for clothes. He predetermined he would only shop at thrift stores. It not only saved him money, but it was harder to find clothes that met his high demand for quality and style.

Nicholas was not diagnosed with bipolar disorder in his teens or his twenties, not until age thirty-eight. But through all those years, he suffered from what he now knows as symptoms.

---

101 Gail Saltz, *The Power of Different: The Link Between Disorder and Genius* (New York: Flatiron Books, 2017), 131-132.

102 Annamarya Scaccia, "How to Recognize and Treat Bipolar Disorder in Teens," *Healthline*, accessed March 29, 2021.

He just thought of himself as inferior. As a teenager, he was overwhelmed by sadness, depression, and low self-esteem, along with regular thoughts of suicide.[103] He constantly learns more about the disorder and treatment options. As a suffering teenager, he didn't know he was bipolar. But looking back, he was showing symptoms: short temper, risky drinking, sadness, feelings of worthlessness.[104] This diagnosis finally explained why he remembers spending so much of his life in misery. I can hardly begin to understand what he was dealing with. But I have been with Josh when he was in a very low state. As an outsider, all I understood was the internal pain can be indescribable.

When Nicholas came home from the structured environment of missionary service, he felt good, and everything seemed fine for a time. He didn't realize how hard it would be. In his words, "You come home, and your life is upended because you're not a missionary anymore. You make some mistakes and then your life is hell again and you're like, oh, okay, I got to turn that around. So, you put things back together, get married, and then you build a life, you build a wonderful life. Then things come crashing down again and things continued to keep crashing down, but you never knew why, or at least you felt like you could always explain it. Mental illness was never the answer. Then one day, you think it was just too long and too many times."

Nicholas now has something to work with since his diagnosis. His medications aren't perfect. His routine is not perfect. But

---

103 Ibid.

104 Ibid.

now he knows what he's up against. He said, "Well, knowing what's going on is huge! Knowing something's wrong but not having any idea what it is was tormenting." He hasn't had a drink since his diagnosis almost four years ago.

His diagnosis came after paying a very high price. It came as an extension of being in rehab. Following a flare up with his back injury from the car crash years before, he began drinking again and relapsed. Before that he had been sober for six years. His employer found out his rehab was not only for alcohol but also for narcotics that were part of his treatment regimen for back pain. After working for years to train and qualify for his dream job as a paramedic, he was fired.

Nicholas found the work of serving people in need to be satisfying. He couldn't think of a job he could like more. It broke his heart, not only for his career but also for letting his family down. He was at, yet another tremendously low point. As he had before, he labeled himself a loser.

Following the bipolar diagnosis and his newfound understanding, he is moving forward. Speaking of God, Nicholas said, "We would love to guarantee ourselves continual ease and comfort. If we were to do that, however, we would probably excuse our greatest benefactor. Because Christ was made perfect through suffering. He has a plan. He has a purpose, and he has turned me into the man, the husband, the father, the brother, the son, the uncle, and the person that he wants me to be through those trials and afflictions, and it's the only way I can become like him."[105]

---

105 Nick Berejkoff's Facebook Page, video, 5:45, October 18, 2020.

In his early forties, it's like he's twenty-five again. Learning to manage his bipolar diagnosis is new freedom. Now, with the help of family and friends, he can direct his path forward through the challenges ahead.

Nicholas said currently people are somehow being drawn into his life with support and insight to help him find ways to apply his experience to lift and serve others. Perhaps his greatest supporter and guide is his oldest son Konstantine, named after Dr. Konstantine Berejkoff who sought freedom by escaping from the Soviet Union. Nicholas often comments how he believes his son to be the finest person he knows. Without judgment, young Konstantine listens to his dad and observes. From the perspective of a child, he provides support and understanding.

In this book you see how people identify, manage, and overcome challenges and obstacles.

The bipolar disorder experiences of Nicholas and Josh have given me a much deeper understanding of life. As Nicholas says, the challenges help mold him into the man he wants to be. Their experiences can serve to inspire you in managing your own challenges in life.

CHAPTER 9

THE IMPORTANCE OF FEAR

———

*"I learned that courage was not the absence of fear, but
the triumph over it. The brave man is not he who
does not fear, but he who conquers that fear."*

—NELSON MANDELA

After a barbecue dinner near the mouth of Provo Canyon, a local
cowboy poet told of a father, his son, and fear. The son was in
his twenties, still living at home. They both knew it was time
for the son to move out and start his life on his own. This was a
minor stressor for Mom and Dad, but from the view of the son
it was a big step to leave the safety and comfort of the home his
parents provided. Had this character thought of all these facts
ahead of time, he might have talked himself out of the move,
continuing to hide in fear, maybe stuck in his room forever.

After a few days, Dad checked up on him. The son said nothing
about being homesick. But he went on and on griping about all

the little expenses of setting up housekeeping, such as buying dishes, linens, brooms, and waste baskets. As a twentysomething, he just moved out without thinking about those things. Also, what about paying for utilities and doing the laundry? The list went on. Fretting over small things could have been a deflection away from any fears he was experiencing.

In his own compassionate way, the dad said, "I understand son how all those things add up."

The young man told his dad he could not possibly understand. After all, his dad was still living at home.

Cowboy poetry and storytelling are often embellished, making common things into tall tales or making the lessons easier to remember. They can be terrifying, humorous, or both. The tradition of telling stories around a campfire was one way of teaching how to overcome fears and learn the lessons of life. Having grown up in a part of Los Angeles where just a few cowboys remained after urban sprawl, I found they all had stories to tell. Even when the storyteller wasn't accurate in every detail, the wisdom of the experience of those who faced challenges or fear came through.

The famous cowboy poet Ed Keenan said, "Some stories seem naturally worth repeating, sometimes as poetry, especially if they can be freshened up with a new perspective or little-known fact. Like gold, the tale is where you find it. Whether it is well known or not, each has its own fascination that keeps the regional history alive."[106]

---

106 Ed Keenan Homepage, accessed October 28, 2020.

Sometimes you just hear the facts. Even when you must face harsh things, things you would never want to face again, they become a part of you. You can build on and grow from the difficult realities of your past.

A couple years before his passing in 2012, several neighbors and I were visiting David Beecroft.[107] We didn't talk much; we listened as he opened up the doors to his past. He explained the hard work of growing up with a family on a dairy farm a few miles north of where we were talking.

His stories reminded me of when, as a teenager. I lived in Hyde Park, a small dairy town in Cache Valley, Utah. The most common topic for "pet peeve" speeches in high school had something to do with milking cows, like slipping on the ice or getting whipped in the face by a cow's tail drenched in manure. The stories were well told and would compete well in any cowboy poetry competition. I learned from my fellow students, milking cows in the dark at 4:30 a.m. in sub-zero temperatures was challenging. Many of my neighbors were dairy farmers. Some of them were in their eighties, still tossing around bales of hay and tending to farm duties. They all talked about the winter of 1947, when the snow was so deep it nearly reached the height of the power lines. I never heard them grumble. I never learned of their fears. I figured they must have always just been tough.

David Beecroft spoke of the harsh and dangerous work he and his family performed just to survive. One fact that really stunned us was from one year to the next, neither he nor

---

107 "Obituary: David Beecroft," *Provo Daily Herald,* October 14, 2012.

his family knew if they or their dairy herd would make it through the winter alive. A blizzard or a long, drawn-out winter could take a devastating toll. There was always the risk of an alfalfa fire or other causes of damaged feed. Many things could spell disaster.

As David was explaining everything that could go wrong, a sixteen-year-old in our group was literally on the edge of his chair. I think we were all on the edge of our chair. This man was a good storyteller. He was teaching us about life and becoming better by facing fear and overcoming obstacles.

This sixteen-year-old was really taking it all in when he blurted out and said such a life must have been exciting! David looked at the young man seriously, slowly shaking his head and said it was hard, really hard. He said it was "a hell of a way to live." He said he would never want to go through it again. But he went through it, and so did his family. They kept moving forward. Their fears taught them what they needed to do to minimize risks. The lesson he was teaching us was the power of courage overcomes fears. This sixteen-year-old and other neighbors with us learned challenges come in life, whether or not you invite them. These teenagers, soon to enter their twenties, were excited to learn wisdom from this old man.

We are designed to overcome fears. As humans, in anticipation of a fearful event, we get cold feet, our heart races, and our stomach is in knots. The Association for Psychological Science reported the conclusions of Professor Jeremy Jamieson of the University of Rochester, which stated, "The body is marshaling resources, pumping more blood to our major muscle groups and delivering more oxygen to our brains."[108]

Today, in our society, facing fears can become optional. The cowboy story of the son delaying moving out is just one example. If we choose to, we can simply exist. Surely, someone will have compassion on us for our basic needs, the physiological needs described by Abraham Maslow: food, water, warmth, and rest.[109] We can shirk our fears and allow them to slowly fester and poison our lives. If we choose to clear out that poison and advance in life, we can only do so by making a conscious choice.

I was fearless before I learned to be afraid. One day, as a small child, I grabbed an umbrella and prepared to jump off the roof. I was in search of the Mary Poppins effect as portrayed in a movie by the same name, which I had just seen in the theatre. I wasn't really brave, just spontaneous. I didn't think about danger, and I didn't even have a plan. There was nothing to overcome except a danger I didn't consider. My wise mom cancelled my experiment in case I failed to cancel it myself. She was my mentor and got me through that moment. Over the next few years, I developed new fears. I learned fear by watching others, always observant.

I watched my friends, cousins, and my brother face the consequences of danger. It was as if I was looking for things to be afraid of. Through observation I taught myself:

---

108 *Association for Psychological Science,* "Reframing Stress: Stage Fright Can Be Your Friend," April 8, 2013.

109 Saul McLeod, "Maslow's Hierarchy of Needs"," *Simply Psychology,* updated December 29, 2020.

- Falling out of trees can break the limbs of children.

- Looking up at a flock of birds on tree branches with your mouth wide open can lead to lengthy spells of gagging and spitting.

- Throwing an ignited explosive cherry bomb near someone's face can cause serious eye injuries.

Additionally:

- My eleven-year-old cousin drowned in a swimming pool.

- My brother fell off the back of the bleachers at a baseball game and needed stitches.

- I also watched my brother crack his head open on a diving board. I can still see the images of the doctor's needle piercing his skin to apply stitches.

I focused on fear and avoided courage. I stayed home from a school field trip to the pier, worried I might fall into the ocean and die. I failed swim class several times, afraid to advance to deep water. When I was ten, my brother pushed me off a flotation device in the deep end of the pool to teach me I would be okay. I immediately panicked, insisting I wasn't okay. I threw a fit and my fear was reinforced.

Water activities were everywhere around me. The beach was a short drive away. Swimming pools were scattered about the neighborhood. My dad, his twin, and my brother swam competitively. My brother Glenn was even a city-wide butterfly stroke champion for Los Angeles Schools. I was proud of him, but I remained an observer, watching from a distance, too afraid to move forward. I missed out on a lot.

By age fourteen, I needed to do something. I felt like a failure. I had to learn to see my fear as an asset, a gift. I saw my fear as a marker that something was out of balance. In the same way fear was a friend to the Cowardly Lion in L. Frank Baum's 1900 novel, *The Wonderful Wizard of Oz.*[110] The lion would not have known he lacked courage unless he first recognized his fear. Fear was his obstacle to overcome. Over time, courage became his new focus.

Variations of a common phrase teach that when you are ready, a teacher or a mentor will appear. That teacher may have been there all along. That teacher remains invisible to you until you are ready to see and exercise the courage to act. I allowed my phobias to blind me from the person who was most able to help me. My brother Glenn (the one with the scars and stitches) had enough. I was an embarrassment to the family. He challenged me to learn to swim in just one session. He would accept no less. The timing was perfect because I was finally ready for someone to tell me what I needed to hear. It was time for action. It was time to conquer this fear.

Glenn explained to me what I needed to do to survive in the deep water. I trusted him. With my mentor standing by, I took in a deep breath of air and a full dose of courage, and I jumped in. Like the dairy farmer, to survive I had to perform.

---

110   L. Frank Baum, *The Wonderful Wizard of Oz* (Durham: Duke Classics, 2012), 61–69.

My heart rate skyrocketed; my stomach was in knots. But as the water rushed over me, suddenly I was free.

Eight weeks later, I qualified for the high school swim team. The following year, with experienced river guides, I rafted through the Grand Canyon over the rapids of the Colorado River. It didn't occur to me to be afraid. My river guides managed the dangers and taught each of us how to keep safe.

Overcoming my fear of water taught me courage means you calculate the danger, manage the risks, and implement a plan.

I'm afraid of rattlesnakes, but I still go hiking. My fear prompts me to know the snakes' behavior and habitat and how to mitigate potential danger. When I see or hear a rattlesnake, I quickly take action to distance myself or protect myself from the deadly creature.

Just as in the cowboy story of the twentysomething finally moving away from home, you will face new challenges and fears throughout life. As a teenager, putting childhood fears behind you, you can look forward to the decade of your twenties. It is full of opportunities to recognize and respond to the actual fears of adulthood. What job should I take? What is my career path? Where will I live? Who will I marry? Will I marry?

Courage is the management of your fears. Without fear, you cannot learn courage.

"Fear is a reaction. Courage is a decision."
—SIR WINSTON CHURCHILL

PART 3

LIVE THE LIFE YOU CHOOSE

CHAPTER 10

CHANGE THE WORLD

"Change the World."

—BEN KEITH

In police work, we meet many people. One by one, we meet thousands of them. They come from an unlimited number of different backgrounds. Each has their own personal history and lives in their own world. We find similar characteristics and familiar behaviors. Sometimes it seems too easy to lump people into categories of behavior and circumstance without assessing the entire story.

Early in my police career, I met a particular eighteen-year-old. Without knowing it, this young man was giving me perspective to better understand many people I had yet to meet, people with common challenges I needed to understand. The details of the conversation have faded, but the meaning has grown deeper and more powerful over the years. He was struggling, reaching for something, but not really. He saw his reality as stacked against him, finding no hope or satisfaction in life.

He was an adult who instinctively wanted purpose and meaning but didn't know where to look, or what it might mean. His history and his environment blocked his vision, keeping him captive in a very real sense. He had no physical pattern or role model to follow.

Responding to his environment, he told me he was just trying to hold his life together. But he didn't even know why he should. He sensed he should have had purpose, but didn't know why. The internal struggle was real. He wasn't doing much better on the outside. There was no one to tell him he would be or could be okay. In our brief conversation, he made no reference to the future, avoiding and deflected the topic.

I attempted to break that barrier by asking flat out what he thought he might do at age "twenty-five, thirty, or..." He looked directly at me and motioned with his hand to stop. His expression was one of fear, fear he might open up and reveal his deeper feelings.

"What was the point?" He said he couldn't imagine he would ever live to be twenty-five, and thirty was out of the question. He was doubtful any of his friends would live that long either. Some of them were already dead or in jail. He feared life more than he feared death. He wasn't ready to confront it.

Though not planned by anyone in particular, the architecture of his world had evolved to completely control and limit his life, to blind him from possibilities. Though hope was ever present, it was invisible to him. It was just barely out of reach, maybe around the corner or on the next block. He was conditioned to tolerate and accept the only reality he knew. His world was a virtual prison. He was in a comfort zone where his only comfort was to be accustomed to misery.

He was afraid of outside input because it was too foreign to imagine. He did not want to hear anything that would disrupt his status quo, his miserable comfort zone.

I attempted to trigger some memory or experience he might have had before he was blinded by his circumstances. I could offer little more than a momentary nudge or a spark. My prayer was at some point he'd perhaps remember something his grandmother said, or some kindness someone had done for him. Maybe he'd remember sometime when he had done something for a friend, or even a stranger, something that brought light into his life.

Just a ray of hope could make a difference in his future. Then, just maybe, he'd be ready to step into the light the next time someone extended a hand of hope. If he chooses to find and accept hope, he can be the one to extend his hand into someone else's world.

While I was working night shift at Brigham Young University, I worked with a security officer who also was a student. He had been through and seen a lot, though barely in his twenties. We worked a lot of foot patrol with a lot of time, learning together as we shared experiences and observations about life. It was easy to get to know him. First off, he was a top-ranked rugby player who had excelled in Australia, Canada, and the United States. That made him an instant hero to me. Before coming to school, he had been working as a bouncer at a bar. In both cases, he had to be sharp, alert, and quick on his feet.

He had been through trying events in his teens and into his twenties. As a police officer, I am no stranger to meeting people who have been through trials. I learn so much from each encounter. In this case, Ben and I teamed up and learned a lot together. He had moved away from his family as a teenager and was searching, sometimes in some really rough places. Along his journey he picked a tattoo. Until seeing his tattoo, I thought my dad and his identical twin brother Merrill had the coolest tattoos, each with his own name emblazoned on his shoulder.

In a moment of inspired clarity to inspire continual hope for a fulfilling future, Ben authored his tattoo. In a beautiful simple script it says, "Change the World."

Ben explained how over time, it continues to inspire him to build a better world, the world he creates and lives in. He said no two of us experience or interpret the world in exactly the same way. When you read a news story about a historical event, it is from the perspective or view of the author at a point in time. Each reader will have their own interpretation from their own world perspective.

Speaking on the subject, British historian Suzannah Lipscomb said, "Yet the truth is, if you take a group of historians working on the same problem, writing at different times and in different places—even if they all use their evidence in a scrupulous, honest, critical and informed way—the conclusions they reach may differ. This is because we are all different people; our context, our formation, our insights are different and the histories we write are personal."[111]

---

111 Suzannah Lipscomb, "A Question of Interpretation: The Public
     Expects Historians to Deliver Authoritative Accounts of the Past, Yet

I saw this phenomenon regularly when investigating traffic accidents. Different witnesses see the same incident, but from different perspectives and different realities. Three witnesses may give three distinct statements. Whether we intentionally change our own world, it is not static or fixed. Often the same witness will have a different view tomorrow or later into the future. What we saw yesterday may be quite different from our view today, next week, or next year.[112]

I met Benjamin Hardy during the time I was working with Ben Keith. While I was learning from Ben Keith as he was processing his life and experiences, Benjamin Hardy became my personal life coach shortly before he moved away to earn his PhD in organizational psychology. The timing worked out well for both of us. He's the one I magically met in the gym. His mentoring and teaching skills immediately impressed me. He certainly figured out where I was in life. Within just a few moments, he could see aspects of my world I didn't recognize myself. How did he do it?

Ben Hardy was the quintessential bibliophile. He read so extensively he had developed an ability to see things simultaneously from multiple angles, thus discovering new points of view and discovery. His reading and enriched perspective in addition to his research into a broad array of materials propelled him to expert status in the field

Different Conclusions Can Be Drawn from the Same Sources," *History Today,* February 27, 2016.

112 Matthew J. Sharps, "Eyewitness Imagination: How Our Minds Change Our Memories," *Psychology Today,* September 11, 2020.

of thought leadership and human transformation. His expertise grew as he wrote and made notes constantly in personal journals about his reading and his experiences. His journals filled hundreds of composition books. Ben's combined efforts helped him analyze his experience and the experiences of others, and ultimately prepared him for his studies in psychology. Not long thereafter, he would become a celebrated best-selling author and leader, influencing people around the globe.

The world Ben Hardy created to this point didn't just magically appear. His teen years were far from what you might consider ideal. His experiences (including traumatic ones) were learning opportunities. As he reflected on the past, he was determined to learn from it and not to let it dictate his future. As he puts it, "Back in high school, I was highly traumatized and confused. My parents divorced when I was eleven, and the pain it created led my father into a deep drug addiction. Over the course of a few years, his home became a dark and strange place filled with other drug addicts. My younger brothers and I lived with my father until it became too unstable and unhealthy to be there."[113]

The three boys moved out and lived with their mother for a time.

Eventually, Ben ended up living with his cousin and sleeping on a Love Sac (an in-vogue piece of furniture resembling a giant bean bag), spending a lot of time just hanging around

---

113 Benjamin Hardy, *Personality Isn't Permanent: Break Free from Self-Limiting Beliefs and Rewrite Your Story* (New York: Penguin, 2020), 12–13.

and playing video games with his friends and came to a point where he realized his life was going nowhere. He caught sight and saw himself destined to watch the calendar pass him by as he languished through his twenties.

Ben was offered a window of opportunity. His church encourages young men and women to dedicate two years of missionary service somewhere in the world. He was assigned to work in Pennsylvania. It was a huge step to taking control of his life, yet he was unaware of the specifics he would experience. He did not do it alone, and he did not just jump into someone else's preprogrammed, off-the-shelf "success formula." His service gave him a new challenging start in a new environment. He was committed to be absolutely the best missionary he could, which meant there was no sulking over the past. He was encouraged by his leaders and he developed trusting relationships with them.

He was invited into the homes of people from a variety of backgrounds and cultures. He literally checked off all the boxes of building a new world, living in and thriving in a new environment.

Then he went to college, creating his path along the way. He didn't just accept the status quo and fit in, but wanted to research and publish far beyond what was expected as an undergrad student. At times he was frustrated with the limitations of an academic environment that encouraged just falling in line with the norms. Actively, he sought faculty that could mentor him into this higher growth potential. I've observed over the last several years as Dr. Hardy has continued to learn, design, and built the world he lives in.

"You are the product of your culture and context. You're the product of the information and inputs you consume. Everything that comes in—the food, information, people, experiences—shapes you."

—DR. BENJAMIN HARDY[114]

Your world is composed of you, a human being. We all have that in common. As you compare yourself to others, you realize you are blessed with a unique set physical and mental attributes, some of which you might consider assets, others you consider limitations. Your spirit is your unique identity, connecting you with God, the universe, and other people.

You are the product of your environment, your culture, and associations. We are the only species with the freedom to choose and build our own environment.

With the past as a teacher rather than a master, Ben Keith and Benjamin Hardy broke free. They built on the challenges, experiences, and lessons from their teens to make positive steps forward in their twenties. In the process they each supported me as I chose to change my environment and my world as a fiftysomething.

With your past as your teacher, you can choose to build your own present and future.

---

114 Ibid, 220.

CHAPTER 11

DEEP FITNESS: FROM THE INSIDE OUT

---

*"Even if you're on the right track, you'll
get run over if you just sit there."*

—WILL ROGERS

I met Josh Wheeler when I was a campus cop going about meeting students. In 2006, he was riding his motorcycle at night on State Street in the town of American Fork, Utah. Somebody coming from the other direction didn't see him and made a left turn in front of him, launching him into the air. His helmet popped off onto the road. In her statement, the driver who hit him said immediately after the impact she watched in horror, thinking his head had been severed and was still in the helmet, rolling away from her location.

His body was broken with much of his upper body, and all of his lower body paralyzed. But he was and continues to be very much alive. As a teenager and into his twenties, Josh was competitive, fit, and athletic. Then his life changed in a moment. But a deep desire to be fit and his competitive spirit kept him moving forward.

Thirteen years later, on Tuesday, August 27, 2019, in Lima, Peru, Josh and his fellow Team USA players rolled out onto the court. After a win over Colombia the previous day, they won Gold, beating Canada fifty-eight to forty-seven. They won the Americas Championship of the International Wheelchair Rugby Federation.[115]

He felt good about reaching out to me prior to completing his occupational therapy in his home state of Oregon. He told me he had delayed his university studies because "some things came up," and he had received an impression I was to become very involved in his life. We met when he returned to Utah to go back to school in the fall.

A spinal cord injury rehabilitation team is composed of doctors, nurses, occupational therapists, physical therapists, psychologists, speech therapists, orthotists, recreational therapists, and other professionals.[116] He was motivated by his competitive spirit and desire to be active through the challenges beyond rehab treatment. I later realized his call to me was part of his guided recovery process to ask for support and to assert control over his circumstances.

When Josh arrived for school, he discovered the apartments he saw advertised as ADA compliant (Americans

---

115 *International Wheelchair Federation,* "IWRF 2019 Americas Championship Results," August 27, 2019.

116 Michael G. Fehlings,"Spinal Cord Injury Rehabilitation: What to Expect," Spinal Universe, accessed February 23, 2021.

with Disabilities Act) were not suitable to accommodate his physical condition. That was a quick call to action for me. I quickly built a ramp and with minor modifications, our hundred-year-old house worked well until he could find an apartment that would accommodate his needs.

I didn't realize it, but I had already been going through training to prepare to be a part of Josh's new life. Another friend of mine had been in an accident at about the same time as Josh. I visited during his rehab, learning about the complexities of the life of a paraplegic and supporting him as much as I could. Being in a wheelchair is much more than just being that person who can't reach a carton of yogurt off the upper shelves in the grocery store.

He shared with me that when you first wake up in the hospital after a spinal cord accident, the counselors tell you directly you are paralyzed with the prognosis you will never walk again. The details emerge over time because it would be too emotionally overwhelming to hear it all at once.

People are not automatically resilient; it comes through great effort and toil. At a certain point in therapy, his support team shared interviews with him of other individuals who had suffered similar accidents and injuries. The interview had been recorded several years after their accident. The interviewers specifically asked them if they could go back in history and erase their accident from history, would they? In almost all cases the answer was, no. They reported if they erased their experiences and associations over the years, they would no longer be the person they are today. As a follow-up, they were asked whether, if they could be healed tomorrow, they would accept a miracle. The responses were unanimously affirmative.

Living a fit lifestyle was still important to Josh and would require developing new skills and meeting new people. The New South Wales Agency for Clinical Innovation was an organization that would validate Josh's approach as he shaped and continues to shape his world. "Successful rehabilitation involves reintegration into the community and adjustment to a very different lifestyle with the re-establishment of satisfying relationships, roles and opportunities to express one's own identity."[117]

After being released from the hospital and completing occupational therapy, Josh was looking for new athletic challenges. Taking on new challenges gave him a sense of control, something that is often lost for spinal cord injury patients.[118] Our friend Josh Eaton offered to team up with as we all learned how to create a lap swimmer with no lower body muscle control or sensation. There was no manual, no website to teach, not a single pop-up ad. The three of us knew what we wanted to accomplish and found a path to success.

We anticipated as many details as we could. Based on our combined experiences, we set him up. We determined right away he was a sinker, meaning his body had no natural buoyancy. To keep his legs from sinking, we strapped flotation devices to his legs to keep him aligned horizontally with the

117 Annalisa Dezarnaulds and Ralf Ilchef, "Psychological Adjustment after Spinal Cord Injury: Useful Strategies for Health Professionals," *NSW Agency for Clinical Innovation,* accessed February 21, 2021.

118 Ibid.

surface of the water. Just a few yards into the swim we ran into a problem—spontaneous muscle spasms.[119]

Just as in all other aspects of life, health and fitness present challenges. We all have challenges in common with others, but each of us must find and build our own path. Health and fitness form an integral part of who we are, who we choose to be. There is no way to separate Josh's spiritual, intellectual, and social life.

Having no muscle control, his legs would spontaneously spasm, bend and curl up, bringing his body to a complete stop in the water. Josh Eaton and I adapted and learned from this phenomenon. We walked alongside him as he swam. As soon as Josh's legs began to spasm, we would immediately straighten them and push to start him back along his way. He was fearless and determined to thrive.

As he networked and met more people, he discovered a sport that could keep him fit and motivated by the challenge of competition. Wheelchair rugby is a fast-moving, high intensity competitive sport played on the same court as basketball. Josh continues to play across the United States and internationally. These days he lives in Arizona with his wife and family and works for the USA Wheelchair Rugby Association. Josh's internal yearning to be fit and competitive has and continues to pull him through challenges. Fitness was his choice before and after the accident. He had new mentors—other players—to teach him and help him develop fitness workouts

---

119 Christopher and Dana Reeve Foundation, "Spasticity," accessed March 1, 2021.

and athletic skills. Then he added his own style to make his fitness program his own.

Fitness is a universal gateway to opening the doors to accomplishing pretty much everything in life. Fitness is a powerful medicine for so many of life's challenges. Overcoming paralytic injuries is just one example.

Immediately after getting acquainted in the gym, a twenty-something—who I'll call Jared—asked if I would be his drug rehab sponsor. After being released from a residential drug rehab program, Jared needed someone to support him and to be there for him during times of distress and to cheer him on as he reported his successes. He needed to find someone he could trust and who would care about him, his transformation, and his goals.

As I got to know him better, he shared past experiences of deep distress. I learned of severe childhood traumas and of the loss of his father when he was a young teenager. After that his life got harder, serving prison time for narcotics violations. After prison, he entered drug rehab. As part of his rehab treatment, he and other friends went to the gym together. He continued working out at the gym after completing the rehab program because, like the spinal cord patients, he gained a sense of control and could see and measure his progress.

Jared's success in the gym gave him a sense of confidence that he could succeed despite barriers and challenges. Years later, he is successful in work and in building supportive relationships. He's another example of a person who finds deep meaning through fitness, meaning that carries into all aspects of life.

I meet people in the gym who are there because they want to gain confidence and overcome challenges in any area of life. With proper motivation and a desire for deep change, they see measurable results. Like patients with the spinal cord injuries, the sense of control offers people greater confidence in all areas of their lives. I've met people in the gym who are working through personal challenges, depression, or trauma, including divorce, sexual assault, and loss of a job or business. Some are confused about life, sensing they have a mission or calling in life, but are unsure about where their path is.

Maintaining a fitness regimen is a lifelong prospect for many. If you start in your teens or twenties, you can build a lifelong habit. As your circumstances change, if health and fitness are a part of who you are deep down, you will adapt. If your fitness regimen is based around surfing and you land a job in Wichita, you'll have to make changes if you want to stay fit. If you are committed to lifelong fitness, you will make adaptations as you age.

Elivate Fitness is a supplier of health and wellness products and product knowledge. They highly recommend their clients provide fitness programs geared toward baby boomers and future seniors. From a marketing perspective alone, this is a valuable market since 20 percent of gym members are fifty-five and older. Spinal cord injury workout programs are designed to optimize their advantages. Programs designed for seniors can also be geared toward their bodies.[120]

---

120 *Elivate Fitness,* "Building an Active Aging Boot Camp for Mature Members," updated February 19, 2020.

A popular local hiking trail was first used in 1906 to haul sacks of lime up the face of what is now called Y-Mountain. The lime was used to form a giant letter Y, representing BYU (Brigham Young University). The giant "Y" is now built of concrete and painted white, measuring 130 feet wide x 380 feet high.[121] The trail to the top of the "Y" is 1.1 miles long with a steep elevation gain of over 1,000 feet. On one occasion at the trailhead, I met a teenager named Isaiah. He was waiting for his grandpa, who was on his daily morning hike up Y-Mountain. As I made it up the trail, I met his eighty-three-year-old grandpa, Henry Miles. Henry has been hiking since well before his twenties. Wherever he has lived in North and South America, he's always hiked, most of the time with his wife.

When I met Henry, his wife could no longer join him because of a medical condition. Henry adapted to an age-related loss of balance by hiking with two walking sticks. He is deeply committed to extending his health. At the time I met him, he had already hiked that particular trail over two hundred times.[122]

In your twenties, you can find deeper meaning in fitness when you learn more about how you can benefit your future health and longevity by acting now. A study measured stamina of twentysomethings by how long they would last on a treadmill. Subjects who demonstrated a higher level of stamina than their peers in their twenties were at a 15 percent lower risk of

---

121 Brigham Young High School, "Brigham Young High School History," accessed February 27, 2021.

122 Jacob Osborn, "83-year-old BYU alumnus hikes the Y daily," *The Daily Universe*, November 3, 2017.

death and a 12 percent lower risk of serious heart disease side effects, like stroke and heart attack, twenty-five years later.[123]

If, somehow, you didn't choose to begin a lifelong fitness regimen at a young age, you will still benefit from activity at any age. One of my fellow San Jose police officers, Rich, had a routine physical at around age fifty. His doctor said, "You're dying."

He had a list of health problems, including what he called a bad heart. The doctor told him he would have to drastically change his lifestyle, or he would not be around much more than a couple years. He had been athletic at a younger age and was a good surfer. He just got bogged down in his work and was out of shape before he realized it. The core solution was obvious: to choose what he wanted to do and who he wanted to be. His brilliant idea, his lightbulb moment, was to take advantage of travel benefits he got from his wife's employment and compete in triathlons around the world. Last I heard, he was still competing in triathlons in his seventies.

If you see an old man surfing Steamer Lane in Santa Cruz, California and you challenge him for surfing in your space, brace yourself. He's likely to call you a punk and tell you he's been surfing there since before your dad even reached puberty. I recommend you don't mess with him.

How do you find the same level of commitment and success as Henry, the former drug addict, the men in wheelchairs, or the surfing cop? Let's look at a few common strategies that don't

---

123 Jamie Ducharme, "Fitness in Your 20s May Affect Health Later in Life, Study Finds," *Boston Magazine,* November 30, 2015.

work; they have only a shallow foundation or no foundation at all. I will leave it up to you to determine what level of fitness you want and how to get there. If you don't have buy-in to your solution, you have no traction and are only spinning your wheels.

SHAME

In addition to fitness being a gateway to opening the doors to accomplishment, well-meaning voices attempt to shame you into getting fit. You hear you are a failure, both individually and as a society. News reports and marketing campaigns heighten our feelings of unworthiness. We are reminded that, as a population, we suck at fitness. Guilt may be a sign you want to find a strategy. Shame as a motivator is only temporary. It is not a driving force.

THE RESET STRATEGY

Each year that same shame leads to the post-holiday sales hype, a seasonal boon to gym membership sales, creating crowded gyms for a couple months. The regular gym goers tolerate crowded facilities through January and February until things get back to normal. Ultimately, half of all new gym members quit within six months.[124] For those quitters, the sense of failure is very real.

It seems natural we do a reset on Monday, after the weekend. That allows us to slack or indulge over the weekend. This is actually sheltering our undesired behavior by creating an excuse

---

124 Arthur Zuckerman, "51 Gym Membership Statistics: 2019/2020 Data, Trends and Predictions"," Compare Camp, May 20, 2020.

for it. If you're going to change, do it now. I wonder if Josh Wheeler was thinking during rehab of slacking for even a day.

In January, we get a clean slate and excuse away our holiday behaviors. A clean slate represents a fresh start but does not provide a solution by itself. Put the slate aside and look at who you are today versus who you want to be, now. Yes, now. Your body may take time to comply with who you are. Your true, deeper self that you chose will triumph. You may choose wisely or pretend by choosing superficially.

Programs and formulas come and go. But if you do not have a profound base, any program or magic potion will only create temporary and transitory results, leading to repeated disappointment.

Brute willpower is superficial and is not even a hint of an answer. Speaking on the temporary and flimsy crutch of willpower, Benjamin Hardy said, "To be frank, willpower is for people who haven't decided what they want in their lives."[125] Don't blame the program or whoever sold it to you. You will only meet your goals if you know what you want on a deep level and why you want it.

GO DEEPER

Going deeper is not a strategy. A strategy is deciding who and what you want to be, now. A deeper understanding of our bodies and our environments can help us understand

---

125 Benjamin Hardy, *Willpower Doesn't Work: Discover the Hidden Keys to Success*, (New York: Hachette, 2018), xii.

what we want and why we want it. Just like a business goal, behavior will only change if you know what you want and why you want it, at a deep level.

Cutting through the confusion of thousands of fitness programs is not easy, and it may not be necessary. Josh, the former drug addict, Henry, and the surfing cop didn't just find a prescribed solution that was handed to them. They chose who they wanted to be.

Simon Sinek teaches that if you know and are committed to the "why" for your goals, you will find out how to get there.[126] Whether you choose to create your own original solution from scratch, take on a prepackaged program, or combine solutions, you will own the solution and succeed to your desired level.

Sorting through the virtually limitless programs, trainers, books, websites, and so on is itself a challenge. Just as we are learning and evolving in our own lives, the fitness industry is constantly growing and evolving. Your challenge is to come equipped with your "why," to design your world and be what you want to be. Whatever your age, physical conditions, or environment, if you know who you want to be and who you want to become, you will find a path to success.

As you've seen in these examples, your greatest successes in fitness will come when you work together with other people or make yourself accountable to others.

---

126 *TED,* "Simon Sinek: Start with Why—How Great Leaders Inspire Action," May 4, 2010, video, 18:34.

CHAPTER 12

MENTORS IN ABUNDANCE

———

"Show me a successful individual and I'll show
you someone who had real positive influences
in his or her life. I don't care what you do for a
living—if you do it well, I'm sure there was someone
cheering you on or showing the way. A mentor."

—DENZEL WASHINGTON

In 1985 at age twenty-eight, I was writing end-of-shift reports. That's a part of policing not typically seen by the public and rarely portrayed on television. It's a big deal and requires a lot of mentoring to assure it's done properly.

Police firearms and report writing specialist Lindsey Berto-men expressed the importance of report writing.

"Police report writing skills are just as important for career survival as any other police skill, such as defensive tactics, firearms handling, and knowledge of statutes and codes."

—LINDSEY BERTOMEN[127]

Part of the vetting process in the police academy rates the ability to clearly and accurately document the facts. Recruits in my academy class who could not perform in this area were washed out. It was one of, if not the, most common cause for dismissal in the preliminary training phase.

As I was writing my reports, a veteran officer of over twenty years congratulated me on completing my rigorous new officer training program. He was really big on training and mentoring. In contrast with the highly structured selection and training I was experiencing, he told me when he was hired in the sixties the last question they asked him in his interview was if he was willing to work crummy shifts, including nights and weekends. With his answer in the affirmative, they quickly assigned him a locker, gave him a uniform, a revolver, and keys to the police car. They sent him out on patrol.

During his first three shifts, he drove around. As he drove, he leaned forward in his seat, clutching the steering wheel tight with both hands. The anticipation of the unknown made it a white-knuckle ride for him. Most cops are good storytellers. He was one of them. As he looked at me, he demonstrated how he was grasping onto the steering wheel during his shifts.

---

127 Lindsey Bertomen, "The Importance of Report Writing Skills for Career Development," *Police 1,* June 13, 2019.

He showed me how prayed with his eyes wide open, repeating the same prayer over and over again: "Oh God, please don't let them send me on a call." His prayers were answered; he had no calls. With that reprieve, it was time to learn.

He needed a mentor, actually a team of mentors. He discovered no shortage of people who were willing to teach. As he became better acquainted with other officers, he absorbed as much wisdom and knowledge as he could. He watched, observed, and practiced what he learned. With the help of mentors all around him, he became a wise and well-rounded police officer. This informal passing on of learning and wisdom worked for him, and for the people he served. There was potential for circumstances beyond someone's training and experience. What if a critical incident came up that he hadn't yet trained for? What if that happened on those first three shifts?

In 1969, the San Jose Police Department hired a motivated young twentysomething as a police officer. Most new police officers are hired in their twenties. This new officer was well liked, but soon others noticed something wasn't quite right. Maybe it was a general lack of judgment. They sensed he had a poor temperament for police work.[128]

Without measurable standards, it was difficult to identify the issues, and there was no justification to terminate him. Still, they knew something was wrong. The year after he was hired, without any justification, he was traveling at a high

---

128 San Jose Police Department, "Field Training Officer (FTO) Program," accessed March 8, 2021.

rate of speed and ran a red light. He struck another vehicle, killing one young passenger. More formalized mentoring and training might have made a difference. This prompted the administration to research and develop a standardized training and mentoring program.[129]

Following the deadly car crash in 1969, Lieutenant Robert L. Allen, who served in the military and had been a staff member of the California Military Academy, developed a proposal for training and evaluating officer recruits. Subsequently, the department hired a psychologist, Dr. Michael Roberts. Another officer, Doug Zwemke, had a master's degree in psychology. They teamed up, and the concept was born for the field training officer (FTO) mentoring and training program.[130] I had the opportunity to become a recruit who was trained in the program, and a few years later I became a field training officer myself.

The highly structured program measures thirty-one necessary behavioral traits. The traits are evaluated daily through one-on-one progressive mentoring. At the very beginning, the new recruit observes the experienced mentor on the job. Over the course of sixteen weeks, the new recruits are trained by four different trainers and given more and more responsibility until eventually the trainer is just observing and evaluating. The recruit must continue to advance and consistently pass in all areas to be retained and advanced to probationary status to work under another mentor for eight

---

129 Ibid.

130 San Jose Police Department, "Field Training Officer (FTO) Program: Field Training and Evaluation Program-Purpose and Description," accessed March 8, 2021.

more months. But the instruction doesn't end there. Training continues throughout your career. This is just one example of career training programs you'll find in many industries.

Alexx Leyva is the COO of Infinity Software. In his quest to save the struggling company, he surveyed his employees to learn what the company could do to help them reach their goals and bring the company back to prosperity. The most common request was for personal mentors. Alexx hired and assigned mentors at a cost of $30,000. But with no specific guide or plan, the investment made no measurable impact.

So, Alexx turned to his own experience. In learning to run a business, he sought out thought leadership and business books. As he brings books in, they become part of his board of mentors. If a book serves as a valuable "mentor," it stays; if not, he tosses it.

Rather than hire mentors, he created an environment to stimulate his team members to want to learn and teach one another. He funnels the best books over to them. As the momentum builds, they continue to learn and expand their reading. His team members started collaborating more and have become natural mentors one to another. Using this "books as mentors" approach, the value of his company went from virtually zero to over forty million dollars.

From the time you were born, mentors have appeared in some form. You have the potential to be a mentor magnet. Even when life seems lonely, somewhere, somehow, mentors are in the wings.

Through your childhood and teenage years, you potentially have access to many mentors. You may know your formal mentors as schoolteachers, band leaders, coaches, employers, counselors, probation officers, and so on. Your natural mentors are parents or other relatives, neighbors, friends, pastors, fellow parishioners, and teammates. Some mentors will be people you watch and admire without having interactive contact.

Many connections from your earlier life, such as relatives or neighbors, notice you are growing up. They become more interested in offering advice and watching you succeed. This list sounds glorious to some, but painful to others who don't feel a sense of connection.

Mentors are trusted counselors or guides who come in many forms.[131] When you enter your twenties, your circle of both formal and natural mentors has the potential to expand, maybe exponentially. Your list may include roommates, professors, advisors, designated mentors, classmates, fellow employees, and more.

I was on campus at BYU early one evening, during that time known as the golden hour, right before sunset. The colors of the sun dominated the view in every direction, reflecting off of buildings, glass windows, and the mountains in the background. As I was taking in the beauty, I saw a college student sitting alone. He told me he felt alone and wondered if he even mattered. From his vantage point, there was nobody in his world who worried about him, cared for him, or needed him.

---

131 Merriam-Webster, s.v. "mentor," accessed March 8, 2021.

He was pondering in that beautiful environment when I happened upon him. He was searching for a life of abundance that included people rather than a life of scarcity and loneliness.

Author C. Joybell C. has mentored many people through different kinds of challenges, including loneliness.[132] Even without meeting this lonely twentysomething, she may have captured what he hoped to experience with these healing words:

> "I am never alone wherever I am. The air itself supplies me with a century of love. When I breathe in, I am breathing in the laughter, tears, victories, passions, thoughts, memories, existence, joys, moments, and the hues of the sunlight on many tones of skin; I am breathing in the same air that was exhaled by many before me. The air that bore them life. And so how can I ever say that I am alone?"
>
> —C. JOYBELL C.[133]

I can happily report today, in his late thirties, the young man I met years earlier at that golden hour is thriving. He is making an impact in the world as he continues to reach out and lift others in his career and his personal life. At that time, he needed a nudge of support to get him through a tough time and overcome his loneliness. At that point he was vulnerable, receptive for a mentor to simply give him the confidence to continue to reach out to others.

132 C. Joybell C., C. Joybell C. Homepage, accessed March 20, 2021.

133 C. Joybell C., "I Am Never Alone Wherever I Am," *Goodreads*, accessed March 20, 2021.

Dr. Jerine Lodder of Tilburg University in the Netherlands researches loneliness. She first became interested from her own experience of feeling excluded in high school. Her research shows spikes in loneliness from childhood through age twenty-five, and again increasing through senior years.[134]

Dr. Lodder felt she lacked the social skills to reach out directly. She broke through her loneliness, bit by bit, through mentors she found in her reading, studying, and research. Mentors don't have to appear in person.

Potential mentors and friends abound if you learn where to look and how to recognize them. They do not always come in the forms we expect. Like Alexx, you may find the author of a book to be one of your mentors. Poets, movie makers, or musicians who died long before you were born may have something to teach you. You can select and hire a mentor or a life coach. You can select a seminar or mentoring program from resources you find online or in publications. Public libraries are a tremendous resource of updated online or print resources.

The late Stephen R. Covey is one of my great mentors, even though my personal encounters with him were limited to a quick greeting on his way to his reserved seats at BYU basketball games. Each time he saw me, he took the liberty of patting me on my head. Our matching haircuts created a bit of a bond between us. The personal connection was a bonus for me. His books and example of leadership continue to have a powerful and lasting influence on me.

---

134 *TEDxGroningen,* "What You Don't Know about Adolescent Loneliness: Gerine Lodder," November 14, 2017, video, 9:02.

Dr. Covey, as a mentor, also had mentors of his own, not just as a teen or twentysomething, but throughout his life. Until his death in his eightieth year, he had a habit of reading about two hours per day.[135] I took his *7 Habits of Highly Effective People* workshop about twenty years ago, and it's still with me. My course instructor said Dr. Covey advised a group of "7 Habits" instructors to read biographies, especially autobiographies, when they're available. He said you can learn a lot from reading about people's lives and experiences. With autobiographies, you learn their deeper motivation and what they felt on the inside.

Mentors continue to appear in life as long as you watch for them or seek them out. They may appear out of nowhere. Watch for them and pray to recognize their importance in your life. They can help you open the gates of the abundance of the universe. Like you and I, they are or were following the path of life. Their experience, mistakes included, brings them into our own world of learning and growth.

It did not occur to Timothy Ferriss he would live past forty, so he hadn't established any plans for the second half of his life. During his twenties, Timothy Ferriss was writing and attempting to get published. At age thirty-two, he released *The Four-Hour Workweek*. Approaching age forty, he was "at forks in the path."[136] To ease the age forty crisis, he decided he needed some mentors. He wrote out a list of questions

135 Leo Babauta, "Exclusive Interview: Stephen Covey on His Morning Routine, Blogs, Technology, GTD and the Secret," *Zen Habits,* accessed March 20, 2021.

136 Timothy Ferriss, *Tribe of Mentors: Short Life Advice from the Best in the World* (Boston: Houghton Mifflin Harcourt, 2017), xi.

that, to me, sound like questions a twentysomething would ask. He sent the questions out to one hundred potential mentors. He published his findings as *Tribe of Mentors: Short Life Advice from the Best in the World.*[137] Timothy carefully created questions designed to help the respondents open up and share their wisdom.

You can gain great insight reading Tim's questions and the corresponding responses. You may find greater personalized advice by modeling your own questions and selecting who in your life can give you advice and inspire you.

Denzel Washington took a similar but somewhat different approach. He thought back to the mentors he found at the local Boys' Club when he was growing up. Then he reflected with gratitude on many more people who had influenced him. He reached out to influencers from a variety of backgrounds to share their stories and to share who their mentors were. He published *A Hand to Guide Me: Legends and Leaders Celebrate the People Who Shaped Their Lives.*[138]

You are not limited to the mentors that either of these authors chose. You can present your own set of questions or doubts to whoever you might select. Reach out to family, fellow students, or coworkers. People are naturally drawn to give advice to or mentor teens and twentysomethings. It would be a mistake to think your need for mentors ever evaporates.

---

137 Timothy Ferriss, *Tribe of Mentors: Short Life Advice from the Best in the World* (Boston: Houghton Mifflin Harcourt, 2017).

138 Denzel Washington, *A Hand to Guide Me: Legends and Leaders Celebrate the People Who Shaped Their Lives* (Des Moines: Meredith Books, 2006), 8-25.

Your abundance of mentors often comes from unexpected sources. Any opportunity to learn from others is a mentorship opportunity. Here are just a few sources often overlooked because they don't involve direct human interaction:

- Biographies and autobiographies: See how real people have faced life challenges.

- Ancestor journals: Learn about the trials and triumphs of your family.

- History books: Gain insight on how we got here and how to prepare for the future.

- Museums: Find inspiration in how people interact with arts, science, and history.

- Fictional characters: Their personalities are reflections of what the authors have observed in the world around them. Each one, whether hero or villain, has something to teach you.

CHAPTER 13

MY PATH IS MY DESTINATION

"The past can only define who you were. The present defines who you are."

—BYRON HUNTER

The utterance "I have arrived" can be a joyous affirmation of a series of accomplishments or a point of ultimate accomplishment. Such feats as reaching a mountain summit or completing a marathon require a considerable investment of time, training, and a lot of hard work and anticipation. Have you reached a pinnacle, something you've extensively prepared for? What's next?

From childhood, David Gutscher was intrigued by the forests of Ontario. He had a particular interest in the Bruce Trail, which was conceived in 1960, a couple years before his birth.[139] His lifelong goal was to hike the entire 550-mile

---

139 "Our History," *Bruce Trail Conservancy*, accessed March 5, 2021.

journey alone. After years of anticipation, finally benefitting from an early retirement, he intensified his training and took the challenge for what would be a twenty-five-day journey. It was much more than a walk in the park. I can't imagine what my feet would look like after that constant beating. I find his accomplishment to be quite impressive.

He did it. It was a rush! David finally reached his lifelong goal.

As soon as he felt that rush, a sudden emptiness came over him. He was so focused on the goal he hadn't even thought about what he'd be doing after the hike. In the shadow of his triumph, he felt let down. The rush was over. He was retired and had reached his lifelong goal. His next challenge was to figure out what would be his next project. On a deeper level, he needed to connect his accomplishment to his path in life. David explained this process:

> "I started by re-listing all the reasons that I decided on a life of full-travel. I needed to be assured that the goal of completing the Bruce Trail was actually in alignment with my chosen path. Did it achieve something of importance to me—personal growth, learning, renewal of my spirit, challenge, exploration? Happily, yes it did. This exercise alone helped to calm me down. The goal wasn't achieved just for the sake of the dopamine rush; it really was important to my life path."
>
> —DAVID GUTSCHER[140]

---

140 David Gutscher, "Dealing with Post-Achievement Depression," *Inspiration for an Uncommon Life* (blog), September 27, 2016.

A couple years ago, a twentysomething friend was talking about how he gets motivated to reach his goals. He showed me some motivational videos that had a common theme. The premise of the videos was to shoot for a goal that is higher than your desired outcome so if you fall short, you will have still met your original goal. I only partially understood what those videos taught. In that moment, the concept made no sense to me. It seemed defeatist right from the beginning.

If I have a goal to drive from San Francisco, California to Omaha, Nebraska, would I shoot for New Jersey hoping to limp my way to Omaha?

I searched a little deeper, reviewing my own experiences, and came up with an example that helped me understand what the motivational videos intended to convey. In competitive swimming, I would stand at one end of the pool on a raised platform (starting block) and launch forward until my body touched and lined up perfectly with the surface of the water and immediately power stroke into swim mode. To do this, you aim and reach for the far end of the pool, knowing full well you're not going to reach the entire length of the pool. You know you're headed in the right direction and will clear as much distance as possible.

Bruce Lee attempted to explain this principle when he said, "A goal is not always meant to be reached, it often serves as something to aim at."[141] Reading this quote through once

---

141 Bruce Lee, "Bruce Lee Quotes: Quotable Quote," *Goodreads*, accessed
       October 28, 2020.

again threw me off. Why would you aim for a goal you have no intention of reaching?

A wise friend taught me how he reaches higher goals when he runs competitively. After weeks or months of preparation, he knows what he can expect from himself. As he's running, he paces himself at an aggressive pace. At different points in the race, he realizes his mind and body have more reserves than he expected. He picks up his pace and exceeds his goal.

Executive coach, and leadership and business consultant Gordon Tredgold talks about aiming high for a big goal and achieving that goal. That goal can be intimidating and overwhelming. He suggests starting small and building up to your big accomplishments. Just as my wise friend wouldn't just one day run a marathon with no preparation, Tredgold prepares for his marathons in the same way.[142]

In laying out your path in life, you may have established alternate paths. Your path could fade away or end, like in the case of a student I met in the 1990s. After being rejected by medical schools in the United States, he enrolled in medical school on the island of Monserrat.[143] That path was terminated when a major volcanic eruption devastated much of the island.[144] Historically personal crises, natural disasters, economic shifts or collapses, and political upheavals force a change of course.

142 Gordon Tredgold, "Secret to Success: Aim High, Start Small, and Keep Going," *Inc.*, October 10, 2016.

143 Patrick Smikle, "Montserrat-Natural Disaster: Life in the Uncertain Zone," *Inter Press Service News Agency*, July 18, 1996.

144 Dora Weithers, "Monserrat Before and After Eruptions (1997)," *Hub Pages*, August 1, 2020.

Sometimes the individual may not even have known ahead of time such an opportunity or career even existed prior to leaving high school or even college. The Silicon Valley engineers who started ROLM Corporation, as mentioned in the third chapter, far exceeded any of the goals they started with. While their goals were challenging and aggressive, they could not see the greater accomplishments until they moved further along their path. As they accomplished their goals, they could clearly see new goals to aim for.

I didn't have a goal to become a police officer, nor had I even thought about it until just a few months before I applied for my first police position. I had a secure job, but when I learned of and researched a career in police work, I felt an impression to move forward, to redirect my life onto a new path.

When I met with the interview board, someone asked me how long I had been preparing to be a police officer. I quickly assessed my history, where I had been, and how my path had led me to that point. I honestly told them I had been preparing my entire life but didn't realize it until about three months prior when I saw my life's experiences had uniquely tailored me for the career I entered at age twenty-seven. The new and unexpected path has led me to a fulfilled life, again preparing me for my current and future life.

AM I ON THE RIGHT PATH?

What does it mean to be on the right path? I had the opportunity of attending a talk given by Ned Hill, former dean of the BYU Marriott School of Management. Students frequently asked about setting life goals and selecting the right path to reach them. He said we may not be assured of a target destination in life or of a direct path to that goal. He emphasized each of us can know and receive a spiritual confirmation we are indeed on the right path. He explained along that path circumstances may change, or we may make new discoveries or find new opportunities we didn't know about previously. So, we must be alert to our own feelings and any promptings we might to receive along the way. Things may change.

Your destination really is more of a journey. You keep moving. Your path becomes nothing more than a small plot if you are not moving. In chapter one we saw psychologist Dr. Jay describe the dilemma of twentysomethings who become trapped in the doldrums of putting off progress for a later date only to find the calendar has passed them by. This gives rise to those who find themselves stagnating anywhere along their path, afraid to move forward.[145]

Near the equator, the doldrum winds are calm or nonexistent as the air moves vertically rather than horizontally.[146] During the age of exploration, ships could be stuck for weeks, depleting food and water supplies. At both thirty degrees north and thirty degrees south of the equator there is a very dry, calm region known as the "horse latitudes." Tradition has it that early European explorers of the New World would find themselves stuck for extended periods, causing them to push their cargo of horses into the sea to preserve water supplies for the ships' crews until enough

---

145 TED, "Meg Jay: Why 30 Is Not the New 20," May 13, 2013, video, 14:49.

146 Jonno Turner, "Seven things you need to know about the Doldrums," The Ocean Race, November 11, 2017.

of a breeze would free them so they could get back on their path.

Being stuck in life's version of the doldrums can be draining. It is common for twentysomethings, like defaulting to being stuck in a relative's basement or being unable to make decisions regarding work, school, or relationships. It's not just a twenties issue; getting stuck can happen anytime in life. If you get stuck, even a small breeze can begin to free you from your burdens, allowing you to get back on your path or to create a new path.

Alexx Leyva, the software COO of Infinity Software who taught us about mentoring with books, has never stagnated, but he has changed paths. He has no shortage of momentum or wind in his sail. He did not intend for his earlier paths to lead him to his current position. But those paths prepared him and led him in a new direction. I've followed Alexx's path through his twenties and into his thirties. With every change in circumstances, he effectively applies his prior experiences to continue his growth and learning. He has built a core self that readies him for change. He gives the same advice Ned Hill shared with many twentysomethings, "You never know what the future is going to hold, but you know the person you are, and you know you can feel a confirmation about being in the right place at the right time."

When Alexx and his wife were living in Thailand, she was teaching school locally, and he was working remotely for his dad's company headquartered in Nevada. The company was having some struggles, mostly stemming from his dad's failing health. In consultation with some of his brothers, he uprooted from Thailand to return to Nevada to help with the business. He had a lot to learn on his new path. Before that time, he was not on a trajectory for a business career. He was an author working in the wellness industry.

While in his early twenties, I noticed how effective he was in analyzing and solving problems, mostly for other people. He was my personal trainer in the gym, and I was one recipient of his leadership.

Circumstances led Alexx to another path of discovery, a costly discovery and physical cost he converted into motivation. As a teenager, Alexx was very athletic and proud of it, but inexplicably he started having health problems. Over a period of weeks, he was preparing for state track finals, got really sick, and suddenly lost a lot of weight. Doctors did not provide adequate answers or solutions. He felt the medical system was letting him down. No matter what he did, he got sicker. With no answers from the doctors, he started doing research, mostly about nutrition. At age twenty, he weighed only 136 pounds.

Alexx's personal unidentified health problems inspired his path. There were problems; he sought solutions. It took time, but he read and studied. He discovered an expert on holistic wellness by the name of Paul Chek.[147] Alexx needed help as his health was fluctuating. Paul became a great mentor for Alexx to continue finding solutions.

---

147 Paul Chek, "Who is Paul Check?," Paul Chek Institute, accessed October 30, 2020.

Alexx was excited and invigorated by what he was learning. He found he was able to help his family members with their health problems. Alexx was breaking free from the limited knowledge base the doctors provided. He continued on this path and became a certified fitness trainer. When I met Alexx, he was drinking a probiotic beverage. Before he even introduced himself, he was teaching me about healthy eating and probiotics. Immediately, I realized he wasn't just a generic trainer, he was an expert and a mentor. I hired him as my personal fitness trainer.

He took a deep interest in listening to and researching for his clients' specific needs. Before graduating from college, he published a well-researched and practical guide to weight-lifting, *Muscle by Science*.[148] It has been several years, and even though he's very busy running a business, he is still my main source for health and fitness advice.

Alexx's business skill did not come from studying business in college. He built on his experience in his teens and twenties. But he needed to learn more about how businesses operate and how to manage them effectively. When his dad's company needed help, he read dozens of business books. He particularly focused and still focuses on a book titled *Scaling Up* by Verne Harnish.[149] Through this on-the-job study, Alexx considers Verne a valuable mentor.

His strategy when working with his dad's business was to look at the entire business in his mind, take it apart, make

---

148 Alexx Leyva, *Muscle by Science* (self-pub., Amazon Digital Services, 2015), Kindle.

149 Verne Harnish, *Scaling Up: How a Few Companies Make it, and Why the Rest Don't* (Ashburn: Gazelles Inc., 2014).

improvements, then put it back together. He considered his childhood when he was curious and wanted to build great things. He started out by taking apart and building gadgets and such. From working with gadgets, he felt an inclination to invent things. He still considers inventors to be among his greatest mentors and heroes.

A year ago, amid the COVID-19 pandemic, Alexx's wife felt spiritually prompted to move them and their children to Hawaii. The effects of the pandemic created obstacles, including a mandatory two-week quarantine upon their arrival. But just as Hernán Aguayo adapted to and prospered from hyper-inflation in Chile, Alexx took advantage of new opportunities that resulted from changes in the work environment brought on as a byproduct of COVID-19.

Working remotely became more accepted. Alexx works a regular Nevada business workday remotely from his home in Hawaii. When I asked them why they moved to Hawaii, they replied they didn't know the reason yet. They are happy and confident they are on the right path, even though they don't yet know the upcoming details.

Shortly after graduating from college, I went to a free presentation on life planning. Although I had a college degree, I still wasn't sure what I wanted to do, or what I should do. The presenter held up a yellow legal-size pad of paper. He said at age twenty-one he sat down and wrote out what he would do at the end of one year, then what he would be at each five-year increment for the rest of his life. He made it sound easy. I couldn't imagine life's progression should be so sterile, as if there would be no bumps along the way or unseen opportunities beyond the next horizon.

I dismissed his suggestion that I should follow that model. I could see little room for growth, for opportunities to learn how to tackle the unexpected, or to need to pray for guidance along the way. I had to find an aggressive, less rigid approach. The yellow pad of paper was the blank slate I needed to structure and plan out my own paths. Writing out your thoughts and goals transforms your creative thoughts and impressions from the spiritual or abstract realm to the physical realm. It is in that physical realm where you put your ideas to the test and learn while you're in the process.

After that presentation on life in five year increments, I wrote out my own strategy. I continue to develop my paths and set new goals.

MY PATHS

That presenter inspired me to create a template for my own dynamic plan that can be modified or changed based on experiences, circumstances, environment, need and inspiration. He taught the importance of writing out your impressions, plans, and goals.

PATH A. MY RESERVED PATH

I hold this unknown path in reserve. It is my favorite path, the most purposeful and the most exciting, presenting opportunities I couldn't have anticipated. This is the path God knew about and was preparing me for all along. This is the path of miracles. This is the path Tim Ballard took when it presented itself. Alexx Leyva was guided here by circumstance.

When Path A emerges, I bump it down to the process pattern of Path B, leaving room for future unforeseen opportunities.

PATH B. MY GOALS REALIZED

1. What do I want? Diagram and brainstorm ideas and impressions.

2. Follow-up research and mentor feedback.

3. Write out goals; make a plan.

4. Grade performance. Did you reach your goals?

5. Assess outcome. Are these the results you want?

6. Am I still on the right path?

7. Return to step one and make adjustments again.

I have outlined a dynamic system that works for me. It fits the person I want to be today and the person I choose to become. My destination is to reach my goals as I continue down my chosen path.

Just as David Gutscher completed hiking the Bruce Trail, you have actually arrived. You have already completed many goals and overcome challenges. Maybe you've completed a race, earned a degree, invented a machine, or learned to drive.

You've reached goals and overcome challenges. Tap into your own experience and spiritual intuition to find and develop your paths. However you track and measure your progress, keep moving to be who you want to be today and who you want to become tomorrow.

If you plan on hiking the 550-mile Bruce Trail, figure on twenty-five days, plus months of preparation.

CHAPTER 14

THE PRIME OF MY LIFE

---

*"My dad says life begins at forty, but I think life begins
at three, because that's when school gets out."*
—THE *HEE HAW* VARIETY SHOW

Societal tendencies lead us to think if we missed the boat at twenty-five then we are forever stuck on the dock, watching hopelessly as other boats go by.

In this book, we've looked at some attributes of twentysomethings, like having greater freedom to relocate or change jobs or to realizing the brain and the body are reaching their peak. This defines "the prime of life," or does it? What if everything you thought about being in the prime of life was wrong?

When I was in my fifties, a pre-med student in his twenties, David, approached me at the gym. He said he was looking for a workout partner and saw we were working out at about the same level. I began to rethink what it means to be in your prime.

Are twentysomethings better athletes? Sometimes. Alex Speier of the *Boston Globe* searched some stats and found baseball players begin their peak at around age twenty-six to twenty-eight and start their decline at around age thirty to thirty-one.[150] David Robson of the BBC supports this concept, stating sports requiring short time bursts are best performed by younger athletes, while older athletes perform well in endurance sports, such as distance running or cycling, often into their seventies.[151]

Another misconception about the prime of life is the predominance of continuous cognitive decline past age thirty. In addition to the research of brain development in London cab drivers discussed earlier, researchers at Harvard University show different cognitive abilities peak at different ages.

> "Some abilities peak and begin to decline around high school graduation; some abilities plateau in early adulthood, beginning to decline in subjects' 30s; and still others do not peak until subjects reach their 40s or later."
>
> —JOSHUA K. HARTSHORNE AND LAURA T. GERMINE[152]

Forms of dementia are more common in older people, but according to the Center for Disease Control, though dementia

---

150 Alex Speier, "What Is a Baseball Player's Prime Age?," *Boston Globe,* January 2, 2015.

151 David Robson, "What's the Prime of Your Life?: Is Aging an Inevitable Decline—or Are There Unexpected Perks to Getting Older?," *BBC Future,* May 25, 2015.

152 Joshua K. Hartshorne and Laura T. Germine, "When Does Cognitive Functioning Peak?," *Sage Journals: Psychological Science 26, no. 4* (2015): 433–443.

is more common as people age, it is not a normal or universal part of aging.[153]

My workout partner, Tyler Evertsen, fits the profile of what you might think of as a typical twentysomething. One day during a workout he was quieter than usual. Then he suddenly blurted out enthusiastically, "I'm in the prime of my life!" He had married his dream girl and was about to graduate from college. His wife had a small start-up company. He had a good job lined up as an IT analyst for a digital marketing company. Tyler had checked all the boxes to keep moving forward. The calendar wasn't going to leave him behind.

After graduation, Tyler dutifully set up his cubicle at his new job. He loved his work team, and he had nothing to complain about. But something was wrong, and he said he just wasn't super happy. The work was simple, and he was getting paid to play ping pong for like an hour every day. He explained they offered him all this food, and the company was super chill. But there was a deeper problem for Tyler. He just didn't feel fulfilled. After six months, he went to the owner and said, "Hey, I'm sorry. I just can't do this right now." He developed the courage to assert his freedom to create a new path.

He soon partnered with a former associate, and they started their own company. He just signed his marketing team over to help another company with expansion. He's grateful for the experience of finding that IT job. The job with the cubicle

---

153 *CDC: Alzheimer's Disease and Healthy Aging,* "The Truth About Aging and Dementia"," updated August 17, 2020.

and ping pong helped him realize he had greater potential by showing him he could better serve elsewhere.

Being in the prime of life really is relative to you and your environment. No matter where you are in life or your physical attributes, you can optimize your potential and opportunities with a "Prime of Life" perspective. I was not at Tyler's level in everything he could do in the gym. However, we each excelled in motivating the other. When we did our floor exercises together, Tyler's form was so graceful he could be on any fitness video advertisement. I just hoped if anyone was watching me, they would feel better about their own performance. However, at my age I was still able to beat him in bench press! He helps me live in my own prime.

Tyler is just getting started. At age twenty-seven, he is living the prime of his life. As he moves forward in time, he optimizes his circumstances and creates an environment to extend his prime for decades to come. His perspective motivates me to optimize my life and live in my prime to fully optimize my potential.

Tyler's accomplishments are typical mileposts for twenty-somethings, but they are not held exclusively for people in their twenties. Life does not end at thirty, nor does it begin at forty. The personal stories in this book demonstrate that throughout our decades of life we each have the freedom to build our world and set our path and create our goals. You can live in your prime at any age. Teenagers have the great gift of time and the advance opportunity to learn social, academic, and business skills to prepare for what's ahead.

Beyond your twenties, gratitude can be your base as you continue to face challenges and seek fulfillment. Getting older actually has its advantages. You can't discount the value of your judgment, wisdom, and understanding. New research is beginning to break down stereotypes of middle age people in crisis. In one study, more than 70 percent of adults, age twenty-five to seventy-four describe their health as excellent. Another study shows people between ages thirty-five and sixty-five report increased feelings of well-being and a greater sense of control in their lives. Between ages thirty-five and sixty-five, and in particular between forty and sixty, people report increased feelings of well-being and a greater sense of control over many parts of their lives.[154]

You are living your prime of life if you are overcoming challenges, building a world you want to live in, seeking health and fitness, working with mentors, and consciously building a path to your goals. If you are not moving on a path, it is no longer a path; it is only a plot. The advantages of twenty-five give the insights, tools, and challenges we need to build our path to whatever fulfillment we choose.

Psychologist Benjamin Hardy is an expert on personality development. He does not see personality as a fixed set of characteristics. He sees it as a choice of who you want your future self to be, no matter your age.[155]

154 David Robson, "What's the Prime of Your Life?: Is Aging an Inevitable Decline—or Are There Unexpected Perks to Getting Older?" *BBC Future,* May 25, 2015.

155 Benjamin Hardy, *Personality Isn't Permanent: Break Free from Self-Limiting Beliefs and Rewrite Your Story* (New York: Portfolio, 2020), 88–89.

No generation stands alone, whether past, present, or future. "Twenty-Five" is symbolic of the abundant blessings and attributes of all generations. Working closely with and associating with twentysomethings inspired me to search for and apply the benefits of that remarkable decade of life.

You see, twenty-five is not about how old you are, it is about your perspective.

Finding My Twenty-Five.

The Prime of Your Life Is Now.

ACKNOWLEDGMENTS

Thank you, Steve Christiansen, for introducing me to Eric Koester. Thank you, Eric, for your inspiration and for inviting me in. I'd like to acknowledge everyone at the Creator Institute and New Degree Press who helped me along my journey and made this book possible. To my team of editors, the art department, the wranglers, and so many more, thank you as well. Thank you, Judy Rosen, for pushing me forward from the starting blocks and onto the track. I'd especially like to thank my editor and mentor, Chelsea Olivia, for always going the extra mile, then another and another. Your patience, diligence, and caring friendship have enriched my life and increased my desire to continue to learn and serve.

To Jenny, thank you for the tremendous love, support, and sacrifice in making all of this possible. Also, thank you for your insight, wisdom, and your years of library service.

I'd like to thank the individuals who supported my book:

Adam Wooten	Daniel Rose
Alexx Leyva	David Figge
Amy Beck	David Griffin
Anthony Johnson	Ephraim Sng
Benjamin Beckstead	E Todd McKenna
Benjamin Diehl	Glenn Beck
Benjamin Hardy	Harrison Riehle
Brady Schvaneveldt	Jacob Major
Brennen Eisenhut	Jane Christensen
Brent Edmunds	Jared MacDonald
Brandon Owens	Jenessa Kildew
Brian Griggs	Jessica Berejkoff
Brian Parker	Jon Sauter
Camden Smith	Jordan Leyva
Camron Wood	Joshua Daughetee
Chad Beck	Joshua Eaton
Chris Udall	Justin Bauer
Colby Gardner	Justin Cash
Conner McKinnon	Justin Stoddart
Craig Retzloff	Justin Zsiros
Dallin McLean	Kai Hicken

Kevin May

Kevin Powell

Lynne Allred

Mark Gilstrap

Mary Kirkpatrick

Melissa Beck

Merrill L. Madsen

Micah Hansen

Michael Morgan

Michael Shields

Nikkol Christiansen

Mitchell Owens

Newton Chu

Nicholas Buttcane

Philip Hardy

Robert Rookhuyzen

Ross Beck

Sam Gillam

Scott Manning

Sheree Johnson

Shirley Ford

Stacie Leyva

Stephanie Hamrick Gould

Stephen Bohn

Steve Goodman

Steve Townsend

Steven Christiansen

Tomas Santana

Travis Hoban

Trent Owens

Trevor Gowdy

Tyler Anderson

Tyler Evertsen

Tyler Hart

Warner Nielsen

William Waite

I'd also like to thank the group of beta readers who've supported my campaign and gave feedback on my writing:

Benjamin Hardy

Brian Griggs

Josh Daughetee

Robert Rookhuyzen

Sam Gillam

Special thanks goes out to:

Baxter Bainter	Dallin McLean
Beck Christiansen	David Zumr
Benjamin Hope	Ned Hill
Ben Keith	Nick Berejkoff
Bill Thomas	Robert Rookhuyzen
Brandon Owens	Ron January
Burgess Owens	Sam Gillam
Byron Hunter	Tim Ballard
Crede Christiansen	

Also, thank you to the many thousands of people who have and continue to influence and inspire me.

My inspiration: Dr. Benjamin Hardy

APPENDIX

INTRODUCTION

Ballard, Timothy. *Slave Stealers: True Accounts of Slave Rescues Then and Now.* Salt Lake City: Rockwell Group, 2018.

Dyer, Wayne. *Manifest Your Destiny: The Nine Spiritual Principles for Getting Everything You Want.* New York: Harper Collins, 1997.

Fry, Richard, Jeffrey S. Passel and D'Vera Cohn. "A Majority of Young Adults in the U.S. Live with Their Parents for the First Time since the Great Depression." *Pew Research Center,* September 4, 2020. https://www.pewresearch.org/fact-tank/2020/09/04/a-majority-of-young-adults-in-the-u-s-live-with-their-parents-for-the-first-time-since-the-great-depression/.

Henig, Robin Marantz. "What Is It About 20-Somethings?" *New York Times Magazine,* August 18, 2009. https://www.nytimes.com/2010/08/22/magazine/22Adulthood-t.html.

Jabr, Ferris. "The Neuroscience of 20-Somethings." *Scientific American* (blog), August 29, 2012. https://blogs.scientificamerican.com/brainwaves/the-neuroscience-of-twenty-somethings/.

Karr, Cheryl L. "Searching for the One: Gardy Mardy." *O.U.R. Stories* (blog), July 17, 2014. https://ourrescue.org/blog/searching-for-gardy/.

Lee, Christina. "2017 Employee Job Satisfaction and Engagement: The Doors of Opportunity Are Open." *Society for Human Resource Management,* April 24, 2017. https://www.shrm.org/hr-today/trends-and-forecasting/research-and-surveys/pages/2017-job-satisfaction-and-engagement-doors-of-opportunity-are-open.aspx.

Lincoln, Abraham. "Abraham Lincoln Quotes." Goodreads. Accessed January 23, 2021. https://www.goodreads.com/quotes/72422-the-dogmas-of-the-quiet-past-are-inadequate-to-the.

Operation Underground Railroad. "Gardy's Story (Part 4 of 8)." *O.U.R. Stories* (blog), June 19, 2020. https://ourrescue.org/blog/gardys-story-part-4-of-8/.

Operation Underground Railroad. "The Team." Accessed March 28, 2021. https://ourrescue.org/about#team.

Packer, Lynn. "Tim Ballard's Mission." *American Crime Journal,* August 6, 2020. https://americancrimejournal.com/tim-ballards-mission/.

Robbins, Tony. "Tony Robbins Interviews Tim Ballard, Whose Mission Is To End..." Tony Robbins Facebook Page. Accessed January 23, 2021. Video, 36:25. https://www.facebook.com/watch/?v=230843514273184.

TED. "Meg Jay: Why 30 Is Not the New 20." May 13, 2013. Video, 14:49. https://youtu.be/vhhgI4tSMwc.

Williams, Joseph A. "When Truckers Shut down America to Protest Oil Prices—and Became Folk Heroes." *History: History Stories.* https://www.history.com/news/oil-crisis-1973-truck-strike.

Woollett, Katherine and Eleanor Maguire. "Acquiring 'the Knowledge' of London's Layout Drives Structural Brain Changes." *Current Biology 21, no. 24* (2011). https://doi.org/10.1016/j.cub.2011.11.018.

CHAPTER 1

Buchanan, Tony W. and William R. Lovallo. "Abstract: The Role of Genetics in Stress Effects on Health and Addiction." *National Institute of Health, National Library of Medicine.* Accessed January 27, 2021. doi: 10.1016/j.copsyc.2018.09.005.

Cambridge Dictionary. s.v. "have a chip on your shoulder." Accessed January 13, 2021. https://dictionary.cambridge.org/dictionary/english/have-a-chip-on-your-shoulder.

Dudley, Graham. "Nearly 10% of Utah Restaurants Have Closed for Good, Association Says." *KSL News,* September 2, 2020. https://www.ksl.com/article/50013227/nearly-10-of-utah-restaurants-have-closed-for-good-association-says.

Gross, David and Sophronia Scott. "Proceeding with Caution." *Time.* Vol. 136, No. 3 (1990): 56–62.

Jay, Meg. "About Page." Accessed September 2, 2020. https://megjay.com/about/.

Karr, Cheryl. "Searching for the One: Gardy Mardy." O.U.R. Stories (blog) July 17, 2014. https://helpmesavechildren.blogspot.com/2014/07/searching-for-one.html.

McKay, Brett and Kate McKacy. "Don't Waste Your Twenties Part I: Taking Advantage of the Unique Powers of the Twentysomething Brain." *A Man's Life.* Accessed August 21, 2020. https://www.artofmanliness.com/articles/dont-waste-your-twenties-part-1-taking-advantage-of-the-unique-powers-of-the-twentysomething-brain/.

Merriam-Webster. s.v. "twentysomething." Accessed January 11, 2021. https://www.merriam-webster.com/dictionary/twentysomething.

Porterfield, Carlie. "A Staggering 64% of New York Restaurants Could Shut for Good by 2021, Analysis Says." *Forbes,* September 4, 2020.
https://www.forbes.com/sites/carlieporterfield/2020/09/04/a-staggering-64-of-new-york-restaurants-could-shut-for-good-by-2021-analysis-says/?sh=2b8fab995dd8.

Psychology Today Basics. "What Creates Resilience." *Psychology Today,* September 7, 2020.
https://www.psychologytoday.com/us/basics/resilience#what-creates-resilience.

TED. "Meg Jay: Why 30 Is Not the New 20." May 13, 2013. Video, 14:49.
https://youtu.be/vhhgI4tSMwc.

Thai-Ger's Facebook Page. Accessed January 27, 2021.
https://www.facebook.com/thaigercuisine.

True Leaf Market. "About Demetrios Agathangelides." Accessed January 21, 2021.
https://www.trueleafmarket.com/pages/about-demetrios-agathangelides.

Turley, Johnathan. "Is This the New Greatest Generation?" *The Hill.*
https://thehill.com/opinion/healthcare/491762-is-this-the-new-greatest-generation.

CHAPTER 2

History. "OPEC Enacts Oil Embargo." *History.* Accessed January 20, 2021.
https://www.history.com/this-day-in-history/opec-enacts-oil-embargo.

Mental Health Daily. "At What Age Is The Brain Fully Developed?" Accessed January 20, 2021.
https://mentalhealthdaily.com/2015/02/18/at-what-age-is-the-brain-fully-developed/.

Nemko, Marty. "Curing Career Fear: Not-Magic Pills for Reducing Career Anxiety." *Psychology Today,* Jun 24, 2018.
https://www.psychologytoday.com/us/blog/how-do-life/201806/curing-career-fear.

TED. "Meg Jay: Why 30 Is Not the New 20." May 13, 2013. Video, 14:49.
https://youtu.be/vhhgI4tSMwc.

Trunk, Penelope. "Why Job Hoppers Do Well." *Associated Career Management Australia,* accessed September 27, 2020.
https://www.career-manage.com.au/uploads/77/why_job_hoppers_do_well.pdf.

Williams, Joseph A. "When Truckers Shut down America to Protest Oil Prices—and Became Folk Heroes." *History: History Stories,* updated January 15, 2019.
https://www.history.com/news/oil-crisis-1973-truck-strike.

CHAPTER 3

Computer History Museum. "Data General Corporation." Accessed January 12, 2021.
https://www.computerhistory.org/brochures/d-f/.

Computer History Museum. "ROLM Corporation, Competing with Giants." May 19, 2004. Video, 1:27:21.
https://youtu.be/VyTuxVQgw6c.

Encyclopedia Britannica. "Hewlett-Packard Company." September 14, 2020.
https://www.britannica.com/topic/Hewlett-Packard-Company#ref92971.

Encyclopedia Britannica. "IBM American Company." September 14, 2020.
https://www.britannica.com/topic/International-Business-Machines-Corporation.

Lasar, Matthew. "Any Lawful Device: Revisiting Carterfone on the Eve of the Net
Neutrality Vote." *Ars Technica*, December 13, 2017.
https://arstechnica.com/tech-policy/2017/12/carterfone-40-years/.

Maxfield, Katherine. *Starting up Silicon Valley: How ROLM Became a Cultural Icon
and a Fortune 500 Company.* Austin: Emerald Book Company, 2014.

Merriam-Webster. s.v. "twentysomething." Accessed February 5, 2021.
https://www.merriam-webster.com/dictionary/twentysomething.

Saltz, Gail. *The Power of Different: The Link Between Disorder and Genius.* New
York: Flatiron Books, 2017.

CHAPTER 4

Dahl, Oliver. "Oliver Dahl Homepage." Accessed February 18, 2021.
http://www.oliverdahl.com/.

Hamilton, Jori. "Why Business Transformation Is an Ongoing Strategy and Not an
Endpoint." Best Techie. Accessed February 11, 2021.
https://www.besttechie.com/why-business-transformation-is-an-ongoing-strategy-
and-not-an-endpoint/.

Horowitz, Juliana Menasce, and Nikki Graf. "Most U.S. Teens See Anxiety and
Depression as a Major Problem Among Their Peers." *Pew Research Center,* February
20, 2019.
https://www.pewresearch.org/social-trends/2019/02/20/most-u-s-teens-see-anxiety-
and-depression-as-a-major-problem-among-their-peers/.

Merriam-Webster. s.v. "BMX." Accessed February 11, 2021.
https://www.merriam-webster.com/dictionary/BMX.

Mui, Chunka. "How Kodak Failed." *Forbes,* January 2012.
https://www.forbes.com/sites/chunkamui/2012/01/18/how-kodak-
failed/?sh=4a1bfa3c6f27.

Penn State. "Time with Parents Is Important for Teens' Well-Being." *Science
Daily,* August 21, 2012. Accessed February 17, 2021. www.sciencedaily.com/
releases/2012/08/120821143907.htm.

Price-Mitchell, Marilyn. "Anxiety in Teens: How You Can Help." *Psychology Today*
(blog), November 30, 2019.
https://www.psychologytoday.com/us/blog/the-moment-youth/201911/anxiety-in-
teens-how-you-can-help.

TED. "Alain de Botton: A Kinder, Gentler Philosophy of Success." July 28, 2009.
Video, 16:51.
https://youtu.be/MtSE4rglxbY.

CHAPTER 5

Maragakis, Lisa. "The New Normal and Coronavirus." *Johns Hopkins Medicine.* Updated August 14, 2020. Accessed September 21,2020. https://www.hopkinsmedicine.org/health/conditions-and-diseases/coronavirus/coronavirus-new-normal.

Steinbeck, John. *The Grapes of Wrath.* New York: Viking Press, 1986.

Truesdale, Ana. "Memories of Chile's Coup D'éTat." *Chile Today,* September 12, 2019. https://chiletoday.cl/memories-of-chiles-coup-detat/.

World Inflation Data. "Inflation Chile 1975." Accessed February 9, 2021. https://www.inflation.eu/en/inflation-rates/chile/historic-inflation/cpi-inflation-chile-1975.aspx.

CHAPTER 6

Contreras, Russell. "Story of the Underground Railroad to Mexico Gains Attention." *AP News,* September 12, 2020. https://apnews.com/article/mexico-race-and-ethnicity-archive-texas-d26243702f11e27b59b591332bb6775e.

Fandom Pro/College American Football Wiki. "Superbowl XV." Accessed March 19, 2021. https://americanfootball.fandom.com/wiki/Super_Bowl_XV.

Frankl, Viktor E. "Viktor E. Frankl Quote." Goodreads. Accessed March 19, 2021. https://www.goodreads.com/quotes/1287210-the-last-of-the-human-freedoms-to-choose-one-s-attitude.

Hardy, Benjamin. *Personality Isn't Permanent: Break Free from Self-Limiting Beliefs and Rewrite Your Own Story.* New York: Portfolio, 2020.

Hay, Louise. "About." Accessed March 11, 2021. https://www.louisehay.com/about/.

Hay, Louise. *You Can Heal Your Life.* Carlsbad: Hay House, 1984.

IMDB. "Louise Hay Biography." Accessed April 7, 2021. https://www.imdb.com/name/nm1026340/bio.

IMDB. "Remember the Titans." Accessed March 19, 2021. https://www.imdb.com/title/tt0210945/.

News 19 WLTX. "Burgess Owens speaks at RNC." August 26, 2020. Video, 3:33. https://youtu.be/2I7_rsUCYc4.

Oppenheimer, Mark. "The Queen of the New Age." *The New York Times Magazine,* May 4, 2008. https://www.nytimes.com/2008/05/04/magazine/04Hay-t.html.

Owens, Burgess. "Burgess Owens Bio-Resume." *Burgess 4 Utah.* Accessed September 21, 2020. https://www.burgess4utah.com/burgess-bio.

Owens, Burgess. "Live Campaign Rally." Talons Cove Golf Club, Saratoga Springs, Utah, September 21, 2020.

Toone, Trent. "Former Oakland Raider Recounts LDS Conversion." *Deseret News,* May 30, 2013. https://www.deseret.com/2013/5/30/20520441/former-oakland-raider-recounts-lds-conversion#the-burgess-and-josie-owens-family.

CHAPTER 7

Eagan, Maurice. Second Chance 4 Youth. "Second Chance 4 Youth-The Vision." December 28, 2020. Video, 4:13. https://youtu.be/SXWjX_t7nT4.

"Law Enforcement: Walking the Beat." *Time.* December 18, 1972. http://content.time.com/time/subscriber/article/0,33009,945166-1,00.html.

Rancano, Vanessa. "A Path to College for Kids in Juvenile Detention." Cal Matters. August 28, 2019. https://calmatters.org/california-dream/2019/08/college-classes-juvenile-detention-california-san-mateo/.

Second Chance 4 Youth. "Homepage." Accessed March 29, 2019. http://secondchance4youth.org.

Youth Law Center. "Educational Injustice: Barriers to Achievement and Higher Education for Youth in California Juvenile Court Schools." Accessed February 12, 2021. https://ylcg.org/wp-content/uploads/2019/05/EDUCATIONAL-INJUSTICE.pdf.

CHAPTER 8

Berejkoff, Nick. Facebook page. Video, 5:45. October 18, 2020. https://www.facebook.com/nick.berejkoff/videos/1893187060822038.

Lake County Record Bee. "Obituary George Berejkoff." May 8, 2008. https://www.legacy.com/obituaries/record-bee/obituary.aspx?pid=111746653.

Rattini, Kristin Baird. "A Short History of Shanghai." *New York Times Archives.* Accessed February 13, 2021. https://archive.nytimes.com/www.nytimes.com/fodors/top/features/travel/destinations/asia/china/shanghai/fdrs_feat_145_5.html.

Saltz, Gail. *The Power of Different: The Link Between Disorder and Genius.* New York: Flatiron Books, 2017.

Scaccia, Annamarya. "How to Recognize and Treat Bipolar Disorder in Teens." *Healthline.* Accessed March 29, 2021. https://www.healthline.com/health/bipolar-disorder/bipolar-disorder-in-teens.

CHAPTER 9

Association for Psychological Science. "Reframing Stress: Stage Fright Can Be Your Friend." April 8, 2013. https://www.psychologicalscience.org/news/releases/reframing-stress-stage-fright-can-be-your-friend.html.

Baum, L. Frank. *The Wonderful Wizard of Oz*. Durham: Duke Classics, 2012.

Churchill, Winston. "Winston Churchill Quotes." Goodreads. Accessed March 29. 2021. https://www.goodreads.com/quotes/721301-fear-is-a-reaction-courage-is-a-decision.

Keenan, Ed. "Ed Keenan Homepage." Accessed October 28, 2020. http://www.edkeenan.com/index.php/southwest/cowboy-poetry.

McLeod, Saul. "Maslow's Hierarchy of Needs." *Simply Psychology*, December 29, 2020. https://www.simplypsychology.org/maslow.html#gsc.tab=0.

Provo Daily Herald. "Obituary: David Beecroft." October 14, 2012. https://www.heraldextra.com/lifestyles/announcements/obituaries/david-miles-beecroft/article_94dad7ff-8a58-522a-ac64-f715d9148d07.html.

CHAPTER 10

Hardy, Benjamin. *Personality Isn't Permanent: Break Free From Self-Limiting Beliefs and Rewrite Your Story*. New York: Penguin, 2020.

Lipscomb, Suzannah. "A Question of Interpretation: The Public Expects Historians to Deliver Authoritative Accounts of the past, Yet Different Conclusions Can Be Drawn from the Same Sources." *History Today*. February 27, 2016. https://www.historytoday.com/question-interpretation.

Sharps, Matthew J. "Eyewitness Imagination: How Our Minds Change Our Memories." *Psychology Today*, September 11, 2020. https://www.psychologytoday.com/us/blog/the-forensic-view/202009/eyewitness-imagination-how-our-minds-change-our-memories.

CHAPTER 11

Association for Psychological Science. "Reframing Stress: Stage Fright Can Be Your Friend." April 8, 2013. https://www.psychologicalscience.org/news/releases/reframing-stress-stage-fright-can-be-your-friend.html.

Brigham Young High School. "Brigham Young High School History." Accessed February 27, 2021. http://www.byhigh.org/History/Ymountain/Yletter.html.

Christopher and Dana Reeve Foundation. "Spasticity." Accessed March 1, 2021. https://www.christopherreeve.org/living-with-paralysis/health/secondary-conditions/spasticity.

Dezarnaulds, Annalisa, and Ralf Ilchef. "Psychological Adjustment after Spinal Cord Injury: Useful Strategies for Health Professionals." *NSW Agency for Clinical Innovation*. Accessed February 21, 2021. http://www.aci.health.nsw.gov.au/__data/assets/pdf_file/0010/155197/Psychosocial-Adjustment.pdf.

Ducharme, Jamie. "Fitness in Your 20s May Affect Health Later in Life, Study Finds." *Boston Magazine*, November 30, 2015. https://www.bostonmagazine.com/health/2015/11/30/fitness-20s/.

Elivate Fitness (blog). "Building an Active Aging Boot Camp for Mature Members." Updated February 19, 2020. http://blog.elivatefitness.com/features/training-insights/active-aging-boot-camp/.

Fehlings, Michael G. "Spinal Cord Injury Rehabilitation: What to Expect." Spinal Universe. Accessed February 23, 2021. https://www.spineuniverse.com/conditions/spinal-cord-injury/spinal-cord-injury-rehabilitation-what-expect.

Hardy, Benjamin. *Willpower Doesn't Work: Discover the Hidden Keys to Success.* New York: Hachette, 2018.

International Wheelchair Federation. "IWRF 2019 Americas Championship Results." August 27, 2019. https://www.iwrf.com/?page=iwrf_news&id=817.

McLeod, Saul. "Maslow's Hierarchy of Needs." *Simply Psychology*, updated December 29, 2020. https://www.simplypsychology.org/maslow.html#gsc.tab=0.

Osborn, Jacob. "83-Year-Old BYU Alumnus Hikes the Y Daily." *The Daily Universe*, November 3, 2017. https://universe.byu.edu/2017/11/03/83-year-old-byu-alumnus-hikes-the-y-daily1/.

Provo Daily Herald. "Obituary: David Beecroft." October 14, 2012. https://www.heraldextra.com/lifestyles/announcements/obituaries/david-miles-beecroft/article_94dad7ff-8a58-522a-ac64-f715d9148d07.html.

TED. "Simon Sinek: Start with Why—How Great Leaders Inspire Action." May 4, 2010. Video, 18:34. https://youtu.be/u4ZoJKF_VuA.

Zuckerman, Arthur. "51 Gym Membership Statistics: 2019/2020 Data, Trends and Predictions." *Compare Camp*, May 20, 2020. https://comparecamp.com/gym-membership-statistics/.

CHAPTER 12

Babauta, Leo. "Exclusive Interview: Stephen Covey on His Morning Routine, Blogs, Technology, GTD and the Secret." *Zen Habits.* Accessed March 20, 2021. https://zenhabits.net/exclusive-interview-stephen-covey-on-his-morning-routine-blogs-technology-gtd-and-the-secret/.

Bertomen, Lindsey. "The Importance of Report Writing Skills for Career Development." *Police 1.* June 13, 2019. https://www.police1.com/police-training/articles/the-importance-of-report-writing-skills-for-career-development-TbzxehM8ZorolzfG/.

C. Joybell C. "Homepage." Accessed March 20, 2021. https://authorcjoybellc.wixsite.com/cjoybellc.

C. Joybell C. "I Am Never Alone Wherever I Am." Goodreads. Accessed March 20, 2021. https://www.goodreads.com/quotes/tag/never-alone.

Ferriss, Timothy. *The 4-Hour Workweek: Escape 9-5, Live Anywhere, and Join the New Rich.* New York: Crown Archetype, 2007.

Ferriss, Timothy. *Tribe of Mentors: Short Life Advice from the Best in the World.* Boston: Houghton Mifflin Harcourt, 2017.

Merriam-Webster. s.v. "mentor." Accessed March 8, 2021. https://www.merriam-webster.com/dictionary/mentor.

San Jose Police Department. "Field Training Officer (FTO) Program." Accessed March 8, 2021. https://www.sjpd.org/about-us/organization/bureau-of-field-operations/field-training-program.

San Jose Police Department. "Field Training Officer (FTO) Program: Field Training and Evaluation Program-Purpose and Description." Accessed March 8, 2021. https://www2.sjpd.org/bfo/fieldtraining/.

TEDxGroningen. "What You Don't Know about Adolescent Loneliness: Gerine Lodder." November 14, 2017. Video, 9:02. https://youtu.be/o4m4DPC1jZY.

Washington, Denzel. *A Hand to Guide Me: Legends and Leaders Celebrate the People Who Shaped Their Lives.* Des Moines: Meredith Books, 2006.

CHAPTER 13

Bruce Trail Conservancy. "Our History." Accessed March 5, 2021. https://brucetrail.org/pages/about-us/our-history.

Chek, Paul. "Who is Paul Check?" Paul Chek Institute. Accessed October 30, 2020. https://chekinstitute.com/paul-chek/.

Gutscher, David. "Dealing with Post-Achievement Depression." *Inspiration for an Uncommon Life* (blog). September 27, 2016. http://davidgutscher.com/dealing-with-post-achievement-depression/.

Harnish, Verne. *Scaling Up: How a Few Companies Make it and Why the Rest Don't.* Ashburn: Gazelles Inc. 2014.

Lee, Bruce. "Bruce Lee Quotes: Quotable Quote." Goodreads. Accessed October 28, 2020. https://www.goodreads.com/quotes/224651-a-goal-is-not-always-meant-to-be-reached-it.

Leyva, Alexx. *Muscle by Science.* Self-published. Amazon Digital Services. 2015. Kindle.

Smikle, Patrick. "Montserrat-Natural Disaster: Life in the Uncertain Zone." *Inter Press Service News Agency,* July 18, 1996. http://www.ipsnews.net/1996/07/montserrat-natural-disaster-life-in-the-uncertain-zone/.

TED. "Meg Jay: Why 30 Is Not the New 20." May 13, 2013. Video, 14:49. https://youtu.be/vhhgI4tSMwc.

Tredgold, Gordon. "Secret to Success: Aim High, Start Small, and Keep Going." *Inc,* October 10, 2016. https://www.inc.com/gordon-tredgold/secret-to-success-aim-high-start-small-and-keep-going.html.

Turner, Jonno. "Seven Things You Need to Know About the Doldrums." *The Ocean Race*. November 11, 2017. https://archive.theoceanrace.com/en/news/10308_Seven-things-you-need-to-know-about-the-Doldrums.html.

Weithers, Dora. "Monserrat Before and After Eruptions (1997)." *Hub Pages*, August 1, 2020. https://discover.hubpages.com/travel/Montserrat-Before-and-After-Recent-Volcanic-Eruptions.

CHAPTER 14

CDC: *Alzheimer's Disease and Healthy Aging*. "The Truth About Aging and Dementia." Updated August 17, 2020. https://www.cdc.gov/aging/publications/features/dementia-not-normal-aging.html.

Hardy, Benjamin. *Personality Isn't Permanent: Break Free from Self-Limiting Beliefs and Rewrite Your Own Story*. New York: Portfolio, 2020.

Hartshorne, Joshua K. and Laura T. Germine. "When Does Cognitive Functioning Peak?" *Sage Journals: Psychological Science 26, no. 4 (2015)*. https://doi.org/10.1177/0956797614567339.

Robson, David. "What's the Prime of Your Life?: Is Aging an Inevitable Decline—or Are There Unexpected Perks to Getting Older?" *BBC Future*, May 25, 2015. https://www.bbc.com/future/article/20150525-whats-the-prime-of-your-life.

Speier, Alex. "What Is a Baseball Player's Prime Age?" *Boston Globe*, January 2, 2015. https://www.bostonglobe.com/sports/2015/01/02/what-baseball-player-prime-age/mS39neFWm4hrVukT6lSYuK/story.html.

Made in the USA
Middletown, DE
10 June 2021

41108289R00119